HISTORICAL GLEANINGS

CALCUTTA ORIENTAL SERIES

No. 6.E.2.

HISTORICAL GLEANINGS

BY

BIMALA CHARAN LAW, M.A., B.L.

Fellow, Royal Historical Society, London.

With A Foreword By

Dr. B. M. Barua, D. Litt. (Lond.), M.A. (Cal.)

Lecturer, Calcutta Univeristy

GYAN

Published by

Gyan Publishing House
5, Ansari Road
Daryaganj, New Delhi-110002
Phone: 011-47034999, 9811692060
E-mail: books@gyanbooks.com

Distribution Network
gyanbooks.com
India, USA, Canada, UK, Australia, France

ISBN : 978-81-212-2462-8 (HB)
First Published, 1922

2nd Impression 2021

Printed at: Gyan Press, Delhi.

Historical Gleanings
Author: Bimala Charan Law

Calcutta Oriental Series.
No. 6.E.2.

HISTORICAL GLEANINGS

BY
BIMALA CHARAN LAW, M.A., B.L.
Fellow, Royal Historical Society, London.

WITH A FOREWORD BY
Dr. B. M. BARUA, D.Litt. (Lond.), M.A. (Cal.)
Lecturer, Calcutta University.

CALCUTTA AND SIMLA:
THACKER, SPINK & Co.

1922.

परमपूजनीय पितृदेव

श्रीअम्बिकाचरण लाहा महाशयेर

श्रीचरणकमले—

विमल

।

PREFACE

The present treatise is a collection of six essays, dealing with subjects of historical importance. Most of them have been published in the Journals and Proceedings of the Asiatic Society of Bengal. I have revised the printed essays and verified the references. I am thankful to Dr. B. M. Barua, D.Litt. (Lond.), M.A. (Cal.), for the foreword, and to Dr. Narendra Nath Law, M.A., B.L., P.R.S., Ph.D., for his kindness in including this treatise in his Calcutta Oriental Series.

24, Sukea's Street,
Calcutta,
August, 1922.

BIMALA CHARAN LAW.

CONTENTS

PREFACE
FOREWORD

CHAPTER I.

Page

Taxila as a seat of learning in Sanskrit and Pāli Literature 1

CHAPTER II.

The wandering teachers in the time of the Buddha 9

CHAPTER III.

Influence of the five heretical teachers on Jainism and Buddhism 21

CHAPTER IV.

Buddhaghosa's commentaries 43

CHAPTER V.

The Licchavis in Ancient India 66

CHAPTER VI.

Buddha and Nigaṇṭhas 76

INDEX

FOREWORD

Mr. B. C. Law, author of the following monographs, has shown me much kindness in asking me to write a few words as to what I think of his writings. Mr. Law, who is already well known to us, needs no introduction. He is a devoted student of Buddhism and Buddhist Literature. Most of the monographs included in this book are reprints of articles contributed to the Journals and Proceedings of the Asiatic Society of Bengal. These will go at once to show that Mr. Law's researches have been confined to Buddhist literature, particularly that in Pāli, and that his is mostly a compilation work. However thankless such a task may appear to the general reader, it has an immense value as supplying materials for Indian history, and to me, at least, it is of paramount importance. Though people talk glibly about ancient Indian history, it is those actually working in the field who can realise how uncertain the data are and how scanty the materials which have hitherto been collected. We are not to remain idle under the impression that there is no further need for the work of collection and compilation, nor should we belittle the importance of the works of those like Mr. Law, who have honestly and assiduously been labouring hard to bring together and publish the references from a particular literature bearing upon a particular topic. I am far from saying that Mr. Law is the first to find out all the references noticed in his monographs and none need be surprised that on certain points our views concur as we worked together for sometime and were interested in the same subject. But I must draw attention to his list of wandering teachers of Buddha's time which has a very important tale to tell. We have so long been under the belief that there were no other wise men in ancient India than the originators of what we used to call the six schools of Hindu Philosophy. Mr. Law's list of wandering teachers will serve to disillusionize many, and convince them that there were not six but sixty powerful schools of thought in existence in Buddha's time and mentioned in Buddhist literature. His monograph on 'Buddhaghosa and his commentaries' is a well-thought-out essay and I hope he will gradually develop it into a larger treatise. His other essays are also interesting and well written. I understand that Mr. Law has taken care to revise his monographs and verify the references.

UNIVERSITY OF CALCUTTA,
August, 1922.

B. M. BARUA.

HISTORICAL GLEANINGS.

CHAPTER I.

TAXILA AS A SEAT OF LEARNING IN SANSKRIT AND PĀLI LITERATURE.

Taxila has been frequently referred to in Pāli Literature as a centre of learning in Ancient India. Pupils from different parts of India used to visit the place to learn various arts and sciences. According to Dhammapadaṭṭhakathā, Pasenadī, the king of Kośala, was educated at Taxila.[1] Jīvaka, the renowned physician at the court of King Bimbisāra, was educated in medicine and surgery here.[2] Princes from various kingdoms used to be sent to this place for education.[3] In one place[4] there is a reference to a young man of the Lāḷha country going to Taxila for education. Lāḷha is the Pāli form of Rāḷha. As to its identification, I agree with Mr. Nandalal Dey who in his 'Notes on the History of the district of Hugli or the Ancient Rāḷha' (J.A.S.B. New series, Vol. VI, 1910, p. 604) writes: "It should be borne in mind that the princess Suppadevī was carried away by a lion at Lāḷha while she was proceeding from Vaṅga to Magadha (Modern Behār), and therefore Lāḷha must have been situated between Vaṅga and Magadha and not in Kaliṅga. The identification of Lāḷa or Lāṭa, the native country of

---

1 P.T.S. Edition, p. 211.

2 Mahāvagga (Vinaya Piṭaka edited by Oldenberg) VIII. 3.

3 Jātaka (Faüsboll), Vol. I, p. 259, Vol. V, pp. 161, 210, 457.

4 Ibid., Vol. I, p. 447.

Vijaya, with Guzerat by some writers cannot be at all correct." In several places in the Pāli Jātakas,[1] there are references to highly renowned teachers living at Taxila and to the various subjects taught there. In one of the Jātakas, a very beautiful picture of the student life of those days has been drawn (Jātaka, Vol. II, p. 277). A son of the King of Benares went to learn arts at Taxila from a renowned teacher. He carried with him 1,000 gold coins as teacher's fee. In those days, there were two classes of pupils—(i) those who used to pay for their education; (ii) those who served their teacher during the day-time in lieu of payment and received lessons during the night. The paying pupils used to live in the house of their teacher like his eldest son. Corporal punishment for offences was not unknown in those days: there is a reference to a prince being beaten by his preceptor for an offence. For the Cittasambhūta Jātaka,[2] it appears that lessons were given to the upper classes only, namely, to the Brāhmins and Kṣatriyas, for it has been said there that two Caṇḍāla youths disguised as Brahmins were learning sciences from a teacher, but were expelled when found out. Of the subjects taught, the three Vedas and eighteen Vijjās are frequently mentioned. The three Vedas are the Rigveda, Sāmaveda, and Yajurveda. The Atharvaveda as the fourth Veda has been mentioned nowhere in the Pāli Jātakas. In many places[3] pupils have been described as learning sippas (śilpas) only, but the word sippa appears to have been used in the comprehensive sense of learning.

1 Jātaka (Faüsboll), Vol. VI, p. 347, Vol. I, pp. 402, 463, 317.

2 Ibid, Vol.. IV, p. 391.

3 Ibid., Vol. II, p. 347, Vol. I, pp. 406, 431, 447; Vol. V, pp. 177,

[210.

In the Kosiya Jātaka[1] it is stated that during the reign of Brahmadatta, the King of Benares, Bodhisatta being born in a Brahmin family, studied the three Vedas and eighteen Vijjās at Taxila; became a renowned teacher at Benares and used to teach the three Vedas and eighteen Vijjās to Kṣatriya princes and Brahmin boys. In the Dummedha Jātaka[2] we find that during the reign of Brahmadatta of Benares, the Bodhisatta was born in the womb of the chief queen of Brahmadatta and was called Brahmadatta-kumāro. At the age of sixteen, he went to Taxila and mastered the three Vedas and eighteen Vijjās. There is a description in the Bhīmasena Jātaka[3] of how the Bodhisatta learnt the three Vedas and the eighteen Vijjās (branches of knowledge) from a renowned teacher at Taxila, and in many other Jatakas[4] we find that the Bodhisatta became well versed in the three Vedas and eighteen Vijjās at Taxila.

In the Bhīmasena Jātaka[5] we find that the Bodhisatta learnt archery at Taxila and afterwards became a famous archer. After learning the three Vedas and the eighteen Vijjās at Taxila, he went to a weaver named Bhīmasena who was so called because of his gigantic appearance, and asked him to search for an appointment for himself as an archer, assuring him that the Bodhisatta would actually do all his work for him. When Bhīmasena got the appointment as an archer to the King of Benares, he was asked by the king to kill a tiger which was devouring all his subjects.

---

1 Jātaka(Faüsboll), Vol. I, p. 463. 2 Ibid., Vol, I, p. 285.

3 Ibid., Vol. I, p. 356.

4 Ibid., Vol. I, pp. 505, 510; Vol. IV, p. 200; Vol. II, p. 87; Vol. III, pp. 115, 122.

5 Ibid., Vol. I, p. 356.

Bhīmasena at once killed the tiger being guided by the Bodhisatta, and was rewarded. On another occasion he killed a wild buffalo. He became proud of his strength and valour and began to disregard the Bodhisatta. Shortly afterwards, a foreign king attacked Benares. Bhīmasena was sent on an elephant, but he was so frightened that he was about to fall down from the back of the animal. The Bodhisatta sent him home and defeated the foreign king. In the Asadisa Jātaka[1] we find that the Bodhisatta mastered the three Vedas and the eighteen Vijjās at Taxila. He was the eldest son of the King of Benares named Asadisa and he had a younger brother named Brahmadatta. His father bequeathed his throne to his eldest son, but he refused to take the kingdom and gave it up in favour of his younger brother. The councillors intrigued. Upon this, he left the kingdom and went to the dominion of another king where he made himself known as a bowman. The king appointed him his archer. In order to remove all doubts about him from the minds of his old bowmen, the king asked him to bring down a mango from the top of a tree with his bow and arrow. He succeeded in doing so by shooting an arrow unto the skies, which came down with the mango aimed at.

According to the Sarabhaṅga Jātaka,[2] the Bodhisatta was born in the womb of the wife of a priest. His father sent him to Taxila to learn arts. He studied arts and paid fees to the famous teacher. After completing his education, he received from his teacher Khaggaratana (a valuable sword), Sandhiyuttameṇḍaka-

---

[1] Jātaka (Faüsboll), Vol. II, p. 87. [2] Ibid., Vol. V, 127.

siṅgadhanuṁ (a bow made of the horn of a ram), Sandhiyuttatuṇhiraṁ (a quiver made up of joints), Sannāhakañcukaṁ (an armour), Uṇhisa (a turban). The Bodhisatta trained up 500 young men and then returned home. The king, in order to see the arts of the Bodhisatta, collected 60,000 archers and he caused his drum to be beaten in the city inviting the people to come and see the arts of the Bodhisatta. He came to the assembly with a sword only in his hands concealing other things given by his teacher. The assembled archers refused to give their bows to him. Bodhisatta requested the king to encircle a space in the centre with a piece of cloth and himself entered the enclosure. On entering the enclosure he put on a turban and took up his bow. He requested the king to invite people of the four classes—Akkhaṇavedhī, Valavedhī, Saddavedhī, and Saravedhī. Then the king summoned the archers. The Bodhisatta gave thirty arrows to each and asked them to shoot them at him simultaneously while he would parry them alone. The archers refused to shoot at the young Bodhisatta. They afterwards shot and the Bodhisatta resisted their attack by nārāca (a light javelin). The Bodhisatta said that he would pierce them with an arrow. They became terrified. Four plantain trees were kept on four sides and he pierced them with one arrow. He was further requested to show more feats, namely saralaṭṭhi (a stick of arrows), sararajjum (a rope of arrows), saraveṇī (a row of arrows), sarapāsāda (a palace of arrows), saramaṇḍapa (a pavilion of arrows), sarasopāna (a ladder of arrows), sarapokkharaṇī (a tank of arrows), sarapadumaṁ (lotus of arrows), saravassam (a flight of arrows). He pierced a plank eight fingers thick, an iron-sheet one finger thick, a cart full of earth and sand, and a hair from the distance of an Usabha[1] by the sign of an egg-plant (vātiṅgana). In the Pañcāvudha Jātaka,[2] we find that in the past when Brahmadatta was reigning in Benares, Bodhisatta was born as his son and the Brahmins foretold that he would be the best man in the Jambudīpa in using five kinds of weapons. He went to a famous teacher at Taxila to learn arts. When he finished learning arts, he was given five kinds of weapons by his teacher. From Taxila *en route* to Benares he met a Yakkha named Silesaloma. When Bodhisatta was attacked by the Yakkha, he first of all shot fifty poisoned arrows one after another. He then used sword and spear, and struck with the club, with the right hand, with the left hand, with the right leg, and at last with the head. When the weapons proved useless, and when he was caught by the Yakkha, he said that he had Vajirāvudha (a weapon of knowledge) with him with which he would be able to put an end to the life of the Yakkha. At last the Yakkha was defeated.

According to the Susīma Jātaka,[3] the Bodhisatta was born in the womb of the wife of a priest. At the age of sixteen, he lost his father. His father was a hatthimaṅgalakārako. When the king wished to perform hatthimaṅgala ceremony, his ministers requested him to choose a priest from among the elderly Brahmins. Upon this, the widow of the priest bacame sorry and her young son coming to know of his mother's sorrow enquired as to where he would be able to learn Hatthi-

---

[1] Usabha is a measure of distance—20 yaṭṭhis, and 1 yaṭṭhi=7 ratanas. Abhidhānappadīpikā, pp. 196, 996.

[2] Jātaka, Vol. I, p. 273.

[3] Ibid., Vol. II, p. 47.

suttaṁ and three Vedas. His mother asked him to go to Taxila which was at a distance of 20,000 Yojanas. The young son took one day to go to Taxila and one day to learn Hatthisuttaṁ and he returned on the third day. He took part in the ceremony on the fourth day.

In the Campeyya Jātaka,[1] it is related that a young man of Benares learnt Alambanamantam (mantaṁ for charming snakes) at Taxila. The Bodhisatta was born as the Nāga king in the Campā River between Aṅga and Magadha. He was very righteous. On a full-moon day, he observed Uposatha (sabbath) coming to the shore out of water. The young Brahmin on his way home saw the Nāga-king and charmed him by his mantra but he was afterwards saved by his wife.

It is mentioned in the Vrahāchatta Jātaka[2] that a son of the King of Kośala learnt Nidhiuddharaṇamantaṁ at Taxila. He then found out the hidden treasure of his deceased father and with the money thus obtained he engaged troops and re-conquered the lost kingdom of his father.

There are many references to Takkhaśilā in Sanskrit literature. Pāṇini in his Grammar mentions it as the name of an important city. The term Varaṇā occurs first, then Takkhaśilā (Varaṇādibhyaśca IV. 2. 82). In the Raghuvaṁsa we read that Bharata installed his two sons, Takkha and Puskala in the capitals named after them. (Raghuvamsa, 15 chap., 81 śloka). In the Rāmāyaṇa it is mentioned that Bharata, son of Kaikeyī, built two cities Takkhaśilā and Puskalavata and placed his sons Takkha and Puskala there in the country of the Gandharvas and in Gāndhāra. The cities were

---

[1] Jātaka, Vol. IV, p. 456. [2] Ibid., Vol. III, pp. 115–116.

flowing with wealth and jewels and adorned with gardens. They were famous for the righteous conduct of their subjects. There were many shops. There were many buildings and seven-storied houses. There were many beautiful temples and Tāla, Tamāla, Bakula and Tilaka trees adorned the cities. Bharata lived there for five years. (Rāmāyaṇa, Vaṅgavāsī Edition, Uttarakāṇḍaṁ, chap. 114.) The Vāyupurāṇa (chap. 88) mentions Takkhaśilā as the capital of Takkha. It has been described there as a beautiful city.[1] In the Brihatsaṁhitā, the term Takkhaśilā occurs thrice as the name of a famous town in Northern India (chap. 10, śloka 8, chap. 14, śloka 26, chap. 16 śloka 26.) From the Avadānakalpalatā by Kṣemendra we know that King Aśoka sent his son Kunāla to conquer the town of Takkhaśilā which was then ruled by Kunjarakarṇa. Kunāla was in active service at Taxila. Tiṣyarakṣā, wife of Aśoka, and step-mother of Kunāla, sent a letter to the ruler of Taxila, who was asked to pluck out Kunāla's eyes and send him to exile. (Bibliotheca Indica series, chap. 59, ślokas 59, 75, 90 and 89.)

---

[1] Cf. Agnipurāṇa and Adhyātma Rāmāyaṇa " . . . . ramyā Takkhaśilāpurī."

CHAPTER II.

THE WANDERING TEACHERS IN BUDDHA'S TIME.

At the time of the rise of Buddhism, there were various classes of wanderers who, in the language of Dr. Rhys Davids, "were teachers or sophists who spent eight or nine months of every year wandering about precisely with the object of engaging in conversational discussions on matters of ethics and philosophy, nature lore and mysticism. Like the sophists among the Greeks, they differed very much in intelligence, in earnestness and in honesty."[1]

The Aṅguttara Nikāya mentions two classes of Paribbājakas. The first class is known as Aññatitthiya Paribbājakas [2] and the second as Brāhmaṇa Paribbājakas.[3] The Brāhmaṇa Paribbājakas were in the habit of discussing Samdiṭṭhikadhamma, that is, matters relating to the phenomenal world, the term corresponding in some way or other to Lokayātrā, the ways of life or mundane affairs. The Aññatitthiya Paribbājakas were interested generally in the question of self-realisation in thought and in conduct, that is to say, "in solemn judgments about human life and the whole of things." In this paper an attempt has been made to give a short account of the Sramaṇas and the Paribbājakas including those who are known throughout the Buddhist Literature as the six titthiyas or heretics.

The term Paribbājaka may require a word of ex-

---

1 Buddhist India, p. 141.

2 Aṅguttara Nikāya, P.T.S., Vol. IV, p. 35.

3 Ibid., Vol. I, p. 157.

planation. It is stated in the Vāsiṣṭha Dharmaśāstra (chap. 10) that a paribbājaka should shave his head, clothe himself with one piece of cloth or antelope's skin or cover his body with grass pulled off by cows and he should sleep on bare ground.

Prof. Rhys Davids was the first to draw our attention to the wanderers (paribbājakas) or the sophistic institutions quite peculiar to India.[1] It is difficult to say when this order of wanderers came into existence. The history of the Paribbājakas is perhaps as old as the closing period of the Ṛig Veda. We are not in a position to describe in detail or with accuracy the functions of these wanderers if they at all existed in the Vedic times.

Thus we may hold with Prof. Rhys Davids that the wanderers were not known much before the rise of Buddhism.[2] The sophistic institutions strictly so called, may be said to date from Uddālaka Āruṇi, the distinguished philosopher, father of Śvetaketu who tried by personal examples to set up a commonwealth of thought in India which allowed no distinction of caste, creed, age and sex.[3]

Although a Brahmin of erudition and influence, he sought after knowledge without considering for a moment the social position of the personages to whom he went to learn. With Prof. Rhys Davids, we may further maintain that philosophy in India up to a certain date was but a lay movement. Yāgñavalkya was probably the connecting link between the past and the subsequent ages. The sophistic activity progressed

1 Buddhist India, pp. 141–148.

2 Ibid., p. 141.

3 Kausitaki Upanishad, chap. 1. Uddālaka Jātaka No. 487. Mahābhārata, Ādiparva (Upamanyu Upākhyānaṁ).

rapidly during the reign of Janaka, the king of Videha, one of the best known patrons of Indian Philosophy. The kingdom of Janaka resounded with philosophical contests held between Yāgñavalkya and other renowned teachers of the time, among whom were some women.[1] But that was in a period of Indian History when the ideal of renunciation had not taken a permanent hold of the mind of the people. Yāgñavalkya and his opponents were almost without single exception householders. Nevertheless it is in the writings of Yāgñavalkya that we can trace for the first time any reference to the two orders of teachers, hermits and recluses (Tāpasas and Śramaṇas).

The period which elapsed immediately before the advent of Buddhism may be called the Samaṇa-Brāhmaṇa period, a current idiom vaguely representing the various classes of Indian teachers who might be classified according to their attitude towards penance, sacrifice, caste, asceticism and other concerns of human life and society. No hard and fast line can be drawn between one order and another, the transition from the one to the other being possible in the case of all individuals. Whether between the Jaṭilakas and the Paribbājakas or between the Śramaṇas and the Brāhmaṇas, the difference was one of degree and not of kind. Without here going into the details as to the points of difference among the various orders of the Śramaṇas and the Brāhmaṇas, we shall concentrate our attention on the Paribbājakas strictly so called in the oldest Buddhist records.

It is evident from early Buddhist passages that the

---

[1] Brihat Āraṇyaka Upanishad, Books 2–4.

term Śramaṇa may be explained in a two-fold sense. Taking it in its general sense, it means all those religious bodies or teachers of philosophy who became monks, who were known as mendicants (Bhikkhus) because of their practice of begging, who shaved their heads clean as a mark of distinction from the hermits (Tāpasas), the wearers of matted hairs, as well as from the Brāhmaṇas, the wearers of crested lock. In its specific sense, the name implies those bodies of men who were opposed in their general attitude not only to the Brāhmaṇas absorbed in worldliness or to the hermits who practised all sorts of penances, but also to some of the wanderers who were interested in mundane affairs. The Śramaṇas were all hostile in their attitude towards Brahmanical traditions. The term Śramaṇa is applicable to the order of six Titthiyas, the founders of schools. The Sākyaputtiya Śramaṇas or the Buddhists were of course in the same predicament. The Śramaṇas were the advocates of strict celibacy. The Varnāśramadharma which signifies the tenets or injunctions of Brahmanism was discredited. Politics was with them but a thing inferior, i.e. foolish talk. The only thing which really interested them was the realisation of the higher ideals of life in thought and in conduct. It may be said that the wanderers by whom we mean Brāhmaṇa Paribbājakas with their various orders such as those represented by the Tedaṇḍikas and others furnished a connecting link between the Śramaṇas who were much absorbed in philosophical speculations (Anvīkshaki) and the Brāhmaṇas with whom, as with the Romans, philosophy was a mere lokayātrā (way of life). Is there any date to demarcate the wanderers from the Śramaṇas? We may here call to our aid some of the Buddhist passages, particularly the passage on Sīlas lending its name to the first volume of the Dīgha Nikāya called the Sīlakkhandhavagga. Proceeding in the light of this interesting tract on morality, we may say that the precepts as expounded by the Buddha himself admit of a two-fold explanation. Such terms as Pharusavācā and Saṁphappalāpa convey a general as well as a technical meaning. It is a curious fact that the term Pharusavācā or wrangling phrases in its technical sense refers to the practice of the Śramaṇas and the expression Saṁphappalāpa (idle gossip) in its technical sense is used in connection with the Paribbājakas in question. It is worthy of note that these wanderers are spoken of in the Buddhist texts in identical terms. We shall therefore remain content with quoting one of these stock passages throwing some light on the ways in which they spent their time.[1]

The appended list of topics discussed by them is of great historical importance as indicating the manner in which the wanderers gradually prepared the way for a science of polity in India.

"Now at that time Poṭṭhapāda seated with the company of the mendicants all talking with loud voices, with shouts and tumult, all sorts of worldly talk; to wit, tales of kings, of robbers, of ministers of state, tales

---

1 "You don't understand this doctrine and discipline. I do. How should you know about this doctrine and discipline? You have fallen into wrong views." "It is I who am in the right." "I am speaking to the point, you are not." "You are putting last what ought to come first and first what ought to come last." "What you have excogitated so long, that's all quite upset." "Your challenge has been taken up, you are proved to be wrong. Set to work to clear your views. Disentangle yourself if you can." (Dialogues of the Buddha, pp. 14–15 cf. Majjhima Nikāya, Vol. II, p. 243 foll.).

of war, of terrors, of battles, talks about foods and drinks, about clothes and beds and garlands and perfumes, talks about relationships, talks about equipages, villages, towns, cities and countries, tales about women and heroes, gossip such as that at street corners and places whence water is fetched; ghost stories, desultory chatter, legends about the creation of the land or sea and speculations about existence and non-existence." (Dialogues of the Buddha, Vol. I, p. 245).

Examining carefully the import of all these Buddhist passages we may perhaps go so far as to maintain that these wanderers, *qua* wanderers, were the sophistic predecessors of Chānakya to whom tradition ascribes the authorship of the Arthaśāstra. It is a well-known fact that in the Arthaśāstra, some schools and individuals are quoted by names, e.g. the Mānavas, school of Brihaspati, school of Uśanas, Viśālāksha, Piśuṇa, Piśuṇaputra, Bhāradvāja, Kaniṇka Bhāradvāja, Kinj alka, Kātyāyana, Bāhudantiputra, Kauṇapadanta, Dīrgha Cārāyana and Ghoṭamukha. The list is far from exhaustive: some of the names such as Ghoṭamukha and Dīrgha Cārāyana are to be found in the Kāmasūtra by Vātsyāyana. We are entitled on the authority of the Buddhist texts to maintain that Ghoṭamukha, one among the predecessors of Chānakya and Vātsyāyana was among the contemporaries of the Buddha Gautama. He was a Brahmin who naively denied virtuous life ("N'atthi dhammiko Paribbājako").[1]

In the Buddhist texts we find that one Dīgha Cārāyana who was a personal attendant of King Pasenadī of Kośala was probably identical with Dīrghacārāyana, one

[1] Majjhima Nikāya, P.T.S., Vol. II, p. 157. Ghoṭamukha-Sutta.

of the predecessors of Chānakya and who was as much a kingmaker as perhaps Chānakya himself.

The early Buddhist texts together with some of the Upaniṣads introduce us to some of the distinguished Brahmin teachers whose views are held to be authoritative in the older legal manuals now extant. It may not be easy to identify the names as given in the Buddhist texts with those in the Kauṭiliyaṁ Arthaśāstraṁ. A presumption may arise that it is not unlikely that some of the teachers mentioned in the Arthaśāstra can be identified with some of the Brahmin wanderers mentioned in the Buddhist texts.

Without however dogmatising on such a disputed question as this, we might perhaps find some clue to the identification of the names in the fact that most of them were not real names but nicknames expressive of some physical characteristics of the teachers. Consider for example, the two names mentioned in the Arthaśāstra, Vātavyādhi (the rheumatic) and Vishālāksha (the goggle-eyed) and compare them with the two names mentioned in the Buddhist texts, Poṭṭhapāda, the elephantiac and Uggahamāna, the sky-gazing. If it be objected that mere similarity is not identity, our reply will be that it does not make much difference whether the names are identical or not. What we contend is that these wanderers were exactly the sort of persons who cleared the path for Chānakya. We append below a list of the wandering teachers with illustrations to show their attitude towards various problems of life, society and philosophy.

The List of Wandering Teachers and their Topics of Discussion.

Poṭṭhapāda (The Rheumatic).[1] Buddha called on him at the hall put up in Queen Mallikā's Park near Sāvatthī, where he was staying with three hundred followers. The subject of discussion was the nature of the soul.

Bhaggavagotta.[2] Buddha called on him at the Malla town called Anupiya. The subject of discussion was the behaviour of Sunakhatta of the Licchavi Clan.

Acelako Pāṭikaputto.[3] Buddha met him at Mahāvana at Veśālī; the principal subject of discussion was Agañña (efficient cause).

Nigrodha.[4] Buddha called on him at the Gijjhakuṭa in Rājagaha. He had three thousand disciples. The value of life of the ascetics was the subject of discussion. Buddha refers to this discussion in the Kassapasīhanāda Sutta (Dīgha Nikāya, Vol. I, p. 176).

Saṇḍaka.[5] Ānanda called on him at the Pilakkha cave at Kosāmbi. Ānanda pointed out that no other speculations than those of Buddha could furnish a true standard of the judgment of conduct.

Sāmaṇḍako.[6] He went to Nālakagāma where he discussed with Sāriputta the question of pleasure and pain.

Ajito.[7] He went to Sāvatthī where they discussed with the Buddha the question of five hundred states of consciousness.

---

1 Poṭṭhapāda-Sutta, Dīgha Nikāya (P.T.S.), Vol. I.

2 Dīgha Nikāya (P.T.S.), Vol. III, p. 1.

3 Dīgha N., Vol. III, pp. 12–35.

4 Dīgha Nikāya, Vol. III, pp. 36–57.

5 Majjhima Nikāya, Vol. I, p. 513.

6 Aṅguttara Nikāya (P.T.S.), Vol. V, pp. 120–121.

7 Ibid., Vol. V, p. 230.

Sarabho [1] met Buddha at Rājagaha. The subject discussed was the value of Buddha's teachings.

Annabhāro and *Varadharo* [2] met Buddha who instructed them in four points relating to his doctrine (Cattāri Dhammapadāni).

Uttiyo [3] *Kokanudo* [4] met Buddha at Sāvatthī. They asked Buddha whether the world is eternal or not, finite or not, whether soul and body are the same or different, etc.

Potaliyo [5] met Buddha at Sāvatthī. The Buddha asked as to which of the four personages (puggalas) Potaliyo liked. He answered that he liked the puggala who did not blame the blameworthy nor praised the praiseworthy.

Moliyasīvako [6] met Buddha at Sāvatthī. He asked what are the phenomena which present themselves to our consciousness.

Sajjho [7] and *Sutavā*.[8] They told Buddha that it was impossible for the Arahats (saints) to commit five sins. Is it true ? Buddha replied, "Yes."

Kuṇḍaliya [9] went to Buddha at Sāketa. He told Buddha that he used to roam in the ārāmas where he saw that some Śramaṇas and Brāhmaṇas spoke on the benefit of Itivādapāmokkha (traditional learning) and some on the benefit of sacrifice (upārambha). The Buddha replied, "I am concerned only with the benefit

---

1 Aṅguttara Nikāya (P.T.S.), Vol. I, p. 185.

2 Ibid., Vol. II, pp. 29 and 176.

3 Ibid., Vol. V, p. 193.

4 Ibid., Vol. V, p. 196.

5 Aṅguttara Nikāya, Vol. II, p. 100.

6 Ibid., Vol. III, p. 356.

7 Ibid., Vol. IV, p. 371.

8 Ibid., Vol. IV, p. 369.

9 Saṁyutta Nikāya, Vol. V, p. 73.

of knowledge and emancipation." (Vijjāvimutti ānisaṁsaṁ.)

Timbaruka[1] consulted Buddha on Karma at Sāvatthī.

Nandiyo.[2] He asked Buddha to explain to him the Dhamma by practising which one can attain Nirvāṇa.

Moliyasīvako.[3] His view was that what a man enjoys, he enjoys on account of his past deeds.

Vacchagotta[4] consults Buddha on some metaphysical points. Again he questions Mahāmoggallāna on the same subject.

Sucimukhī[5] questions Sāriputta at Rājagaha on modes of eating.

Susīma[6] interviews at Rājagaha the Bhikkhus who had just attained Arahatship.

Uggāhamāno[7] was in the Mallikārāma at Ekasālaka. He met Pañcakaṅga Thapati on his way to Jetavana and discussed with him about the perfect man.

Pilotiko[8] met Jānussoni Brahmin on his way from Jetavana. He asked him about the knowledge of the Buddha who replied that it was beyond his power to measure the knowledge of Buddha.

Potaliputta[9] met Samiddhi, a Bhikkhu. He told him that he heard from the Buddha that kāya and vacikammas were no true actions. Volition of deliberate action is the action in the true sense of the term.

Sakuladāyi.[10] He was staying at Veluvana at Rājagaha

---

1 Saṁyutta Nikāya (P.T.S.), pt. II, p. 22.

2 Ibid., Vol. V, p. 11. 3 Ibid., Vol. IV, p. 230.

4 Saṁyutta Nikāya, Vol. III, p. 257; Ibid., Vol. IV, pp. 398 and 401.

5 Ibid., Vol. III, pp. 238–240. 6 Ibid., Vol. II, pp. 119–128.

7 Majjhima Nikāya, Vol. II, p. 22.

8 Ibid., Vol. I, p. 175. 9 Ibid., Vol. III, p. 207.

10 Ibid., Vol. II, pp. 1–22.

in company with many distinguished wanderers like Varadhara, Annabhāra and others. He informed Buddha that in the past Aṅga and Magadha were seething with sophistic activities.

Cūlasakuladāyi.[1] Buddha called on him at Veluvana in Rājagaha. He calls himself a follower of Nigaṇṭha Nāthaputta. Buddha tried to impress on him that the observance of the five moral precepts and the practice of penance were not enough for realisation of Summum Bonum.

Vekhanassa.[2] The subject of discussion of this wanderer was paramavaṇṇoattā, 'soul in its height of purity.'

Vacchagotta.[3] Buddha met him at Mahāvana at Vesālī. Vacchagotta enquired whether it was possible for a householder to attain immortality. On another occasion, his enquiry consisted of some ontological problems, e.g. whether the world is eternal or not. (Majjhima Nikāya, Vol. I, pp. 483–489.) On another occasion Vacchagotta held a discussion with the Buddha on some questions relating to ethics.

Dīghanakha[4] (Long Nailed) met him at Gijjhakuṭa at Rājagaha. He is said to have held this view 'nothing of me abides.' ('Sabbam me na khamati.')

Māgandiya.[5] He spoke of Buddha in an opprobrious term as Bhūnahu (Brunahan). Cf. Isopaniṣad in which the Vājasaneyas speak of some of unknown opponents who were perhaps unmarried recluses as ātmahanojanā.

---

1 Majjhima Nikāya, Vol. II, pp. 29–39.

2 Ibid., Vol. II, pp. 40–44.

3 Ibid., Vol. I, p. 481.

4 Ibid., Vol. I, p. 497.

5 Ibid., Vol. I, p. 501, Sutta-Nipāta, p. 163.

The Vājasaneyas regard their opponents' modes of life as suicidal.

Sabhiyo[1] informed Buddha that the six distinguished Tīrthakaras, Pūraṇa Kassapa and others were senior to Buddha in age. But the latter contended that seniority goes not by age but by wisdom.

[1] Sutta-Nipāta, p. 91.

CHAPTER III.

INFLUENCE OF THE FIVE HERETICAL TEACHERS ON JAINISM AND BUDDHISM.

It is still an open question whether an extensive research can be instituted with regard to the influence which the doctrines of the five heretical teachers exercised on the development of Jainism and Buddhism, seeing that the evidentiary material on the subject is very meagre. So far as I can recollect, it was Prof. Max Muller who first tried to assign a definite position to them in the history of the six systems of Indian Philosophy. With all deference to that great scholar, I must say that he has hardly succeeded in establishing the precise position which these teachers occupy in the history of the six systems of Indian Philosophy or in that of Jainism and Buddhism. A short account of the six heretical teachers (including Mahāvīra) appears in Rockhill's Life of the Buddha [1] drawn from the Tibetan translation of the Sāmaññaphala Sutta. Mr. Rockhill gives in his Appendix extracts from the Jaina Bhagavatī XV. on the intercourse between Mahāvīra (Nigaṇṭha Nāthaputta) and Gosāla Maṅkhaliputta, and also an account of the doctrines of the six heretical teachers according to two Chinese versions of the Sāmaññaphala Sutta. But he too does not endeavour to solve the real question at issue. The same remark applies to Spence Hardy, Dr. Oldenberg, and other writers on Buddhism who have been content with furnishing us with a mere legendary account of them. Prof. Jacobi in his Introduction to

[1] pp. 100–105.

the Gaina Sūtras, pt. II, p. xxvii f. n., is the first to call our attention to the great importance of these teachers. "The records of the Buddhists and Jainas about the philosophic ideas current at the time of the Buddha and Mahāvīra, meagre though they be, are of the greatest importance to the historian of that epoch. For they show us the ground on which and the materials with which, the great religious reformers had to build their systems. The considerable similarity between some of these heretical doctrines on one side and Jaina or Buddhist ideas on the other, is very suggestive, and it favours the assumption that the Buddha as well as Mahāvīra owed some of their conceptions to these very heretics." Alluding to these significant words of Prof. Jacobi, Dr. Rhys Davids remarks, "the philosophical and religious speculations contained in them (that is, the Buddhist and Jaina records) may not have the originality, or intrinsic value, either of the Vedānta or of Buddhism. But they are none the less historically important because they give evidence of a stage less cultured, more animistic, that is to say, earlier. And incidentally they will undoubtedly be found, as the portions accessible already show to contain a large number of important references to the ancient geography, the political divisions, the social and economic conditions of India at a period hitherto very imperfectly understood."[1]

Besides Prof. Jacobi, we must also mention Mrs. Rhys Davids who has made a very serious attempt to discuss how these teachers prepared the way even through their sophistry for the great Buddha. The Buddhist records earlier as well as later abound in incidental references

[1] Buddhist India (Rhys Davids), pp. 163–164.

to a number of teachers mentioned promiscuously as the six Titthiyas or Tīrthikas. Some of these records can hardly bear the scrutiny of critical research, in as much as they tell us in various ways that the fame of these teachers faded away before the rising glory and dazzling brilliance of Buddha's career. For instance in the Jātaka,[1] these teachers are contrasted with Buddha Gautama as a filthy crow in comparison with the painted, well-trained and sweet-voiced peacock.

Milinda Pañho, (the Questions of King Milinda), which can be dated the second century of the Christian era, contains a spurious account of the six Titthiyas which leads us back to the Sāmaññaphala Sutta that might be taken as the most typical of genuine Buddhist fragments. Meagre as the account in the Sutta is, and as there is a great possibility of misconception on the part of the writers about their opponents' views, we must be careful not to come to a conclusion on the basis of the Sāmaññaphala Sutta alone. That is to say, its evidence must be accepted with due care and we must see that it tallies with other passages contained in the Canon. Of the six teachers, Jaina Aṅgas unfortunately only mention Makkhali Gosālaputta and Nigaṇṭha Nāthaputta (identified with Mahāvīra). But there are striking passages here and there embodying the doctrines of the teachers though their names are not expressly mentioned.

In the Sāmaññaphala Sutta and other older Buddhist Suttas, the six teachers are spoken of in identical terms as "the head of an order, of a following, the teacher of a school, well known and of repute as a sophist, revered by the people, a man of experience who has long been

[1] Jātaka (Faüsboll), No. 339, Vol. III, pp. 126–128.

a recluse, old, and well-striken in years." (Dialogues of the Buddha, S.B.B., Vol. II, p. 66).

The Mahāsakuladāyī Sutta of the Majjhima Nikāya[1] alludes to Magadha as seething with speculative fervour stirred up by these Titthiyas. The same Sutta points out that the disciples of these teachers carried on philosophical discussions with the indomitable energy and boldness characterising the spirit of the age. In spite of the general tendency of the Jaina works to paint Gosala in dark colours, the Bhagavatī had to admit that Gosāla attained Jinahood and that he was recognised as a teacher at Sāvatthī some two years before Mahāvīra. In the Sabhiya Sutta of the Suttanipāta,[2] a wandering teacher named Sabhiya asked Buddha if he was younger in age than the six distinguished teachers and junior to them by renunciation. Samaṇa Gotama simply evaded the question by telling the wanderer that seniority went by wisdom and not by age. But we have another important passage which definitely states the fact that the Samaṇa Gotama was a younger contemporary of these six teachers.

The Sāmagāma Sutta of the Majjhima Nikāya[3] and the Pāṭika Sutta of the Dīgha Nikāya (Vol. III) testify to the fact that Nigaṇṭha Nāthaputta or Mahāvīra predeceased Buddha by a few years. Dr. Hoernle conjectures that Mahāvīra died some five years before the Buddha.[4] It follows from the evidence of the Abhayarājakumāra Sutta[5] of the Majjhima Nikāya that Mahāvīra was aware of the fact of dissension between Buddha

---

[1] p. 2, Vol. II (P.T.S.).

[2] p. 91 (P.T.S.).

[3] Vol. II (P.T.S.), p. 243.

[4] Ājivikas, Hastings' Encyclopaedia of Religion and Ethics.

[5] Majjhima Nikāya, Vol. I, p. 392.

and Devadatta. In the opinion of Prof. Kern, the death of Bimbisāra took place when Buddha had reached the age of seventy-two, and that Devadatta's agitation against the Buddha must be dated some time after this event.[1] Judging from the documentary evidence Dr. Hoernle's conjectures would seem to have substantial historical accuracy. Mahāvīra is said to have lived seventy-two years and Buddha is said to have died at the age of eighty. Thus the greater part of Mahāvīra's life coincides with that of Buddha. After carefully examining the data supplied by the Jaina records, Dr. Hoernle has come to the conclusion that Gosāla Maṅkhaliputta had become a far-famed teacher some two years before Mahāvīra and that the latter survived the former by sixteen years.[2]

Notwithstanding persistent insinuation as to Gosāla being formerly a disciple of Mahāvīra and as to his rupture with his teacher, there is room for doubt if Gosāla had ever been a disciple of Mahāvīra. While the malicious Jaina accounts deepened the mystery about the relation between the two teachers, we may have recourse to the Buddhist writings for more reliable information. The Buddhist fragments are unanimous in referring to them as the most distinguished sophists of the time, the recognised founders of the two separate schools namely the Ājivikas or Maskarins and the Nigaṇṭhas (Jainas).

To the important question as to what was the precise relationship between the two teachers we shall return later. At this stage of our enquiry we can safely assert

1 Kern's Indian Buddhism, pp. 38–39.

2 Uvāsagadasāo, Tr. pp. 110–111.

that Makkhali Gosāla was one of the older contemporaries of Mahāvīra. As regards the remaining four sophists, it is not very easy to determine their dates. On the authority of the Buddhist Suttas we can say no more than that they were all amongst the older contemporaries of Buddha Gotama. There are, however, a few passages in the Buddhist Canon which furnish us with a clue to the date of Sañjaya of the Belaṭṭhi clan. The Buddhist Suttas make mention of Sañjaya Belaṭṭhiputta, and of a wanderer named Sañjaya. The former is counted among the six heretical teachers or Aññatitthiya Paribbājakas, that is, the sophists belonging to other schools, and the latter is alluded to as the previous teacher of Sāriputta and Moggallāna who became, later on, the chief disciples of Buddha Gotama. On a close examination of the import of some Buddhist passages of the Aṅguttara Nikāya it seems very probable that Sañjaya Belaṭṭhiputta was the same person as Sañjaya the wanderer. It is needless to add that Drs. Kern and Jacobi are of the same opinion on this point.[1] If so, it follows that Sañjaya died shortly after the time when Sāriputta and Moggallāna had joined (along with many disciples of Sañjaya, their former teacher) the Buddhist order in the second year of Buddha's career as a teacher, that is, in the 37th year of Buddha's life. Of course, we have evidence to prove that though Sañjaya predeceased Buddha, a school survived at least up till the reign of King Aśoka.

Thus we see that Sañjaya was an older contemporary not only of Buddha but also of Mahāvīra and Makkhali Gosāla.

---

[1] Kern's Indian Buddhism, p. 32.

A Kavandhin Kātyāyana is mentioned in the Prasnopanishat as a younger contemporary of Pippalāda to whom we owe an outline of the Sāṅkhya system of Philosophy.[1]

The nickname Kavandhin applied to the name of Kātyāyana is of some interest. Kavandhin or Kukuda was really a nickname intended to distinguish the famous sophist from other teachers bearing his name.

Supposing that Kukuda Kātyāyana or Kavandhin Kātyāyana was a younger contemporary of Pipallāda and that the Buddha was a younger contemporary of Kātyāyana, it does not seem improbable that Kātyāyana was of the same age as Sañjaya. Prof. Kern relates a legend to the effect that Pūraṇa Kassapa committed suicide by throwing himself into the river with a large jar tied to his neck some time in the 42nd year of Buddha's life.[2] We have reason to believe that Ajitakesakambalī was of the same age as Kukuda Kātyāyana. The series of dates here suggested must be regarded as provisional and tentative. It must be established by corroborative evidence of the interconnection of the doctrines of these six renowned sophists. It is of little importance whether one teacher was born or died a few years earlier or later than another. What is of real importance to the historian is the proof that these teachers in spite of their divergences belonged to the same period of thought-development in India and prepared the way for the doctrine of Buddha.

It may be of some interest to note that the Buddhist attitude towards Mahāvīra and his doctrine was not so

1 Praśnopanishat, Pras. I. I.

2 Kern's Indian Buddhism, p. 33.

hostile as in the case of his predecessors. Buddhaghosa, the celebrated Buddhist commentator, goes so far as to suggest that Mahāvīra's doctrine of Cātuyāma Saṁvara (four-fold restraint) has some good points in it. I am told by my friend Dr. B. M. Barua, M.A., D.Litt. (London), that Dr. F. W. Thomas is inclined to assign to Mahāvīra the same position in relation to five earlier wandering teachers as Socrates stands in relation to the Greek sophists. Leaving aside for the moment the question as to whether Mahāvīra can be thus separated from his sophistic predecessors, it is important to observe that the Buddhists distinguish these six teachers in a body from other wandering teachers of the time, as the Aññatitthiya paribbājakas from the Brahmin Paribbājakas.[1]

The Buddhist word Pharusavācā can, of course, supply a criterion by which we can distinguish two classes of paribbājakas. It is in reference to the six schools of philosophy and to these alone that Buddha and his contemporaries said that they were in the habit of exchanging wrangling phrases in the heat of philosophic discussion. "You don't understand this doctrine and discipline. I do. How should you know about this doctrine and discipline? You have fallen into wrong views. It is I who am right."[2] We know nothing about the lives of these teachers. All that we know about them is that they were all recluses (samaṇas), shavelings (muṇḍakas), and wanderers (paribbājakas). They distinguished themselves from the hermits on one side, and from the Brahmin householders on the other.

---

[1] See my paper "A short account of the wandering teachers at the time of the Buddha." (J.A.S.B., New Series, Vol. XIV, 1918, No. 7.)

[2] Majjhima Nikāya, Vol. II, p. 17.

Thus they formed a connecting link between the ascetics practising penances and austerities in the forest and the Brahmin teachers engrossed in worldly affairs. They were, as a rule, all bachelors and cut asunder all worldly ties, but they were not like the ascetics who were entirely out of touch with the civic society. As a matter of fact their headquarters were established generally in the vicinity of a royal capital outside the city wall. They differed in intelligence, temperament, character, and outlook. Taking the ascetic and the Brahmin householder to represent the two extremes, these teachers can be placed either in an ascending or in a descending order ; ascending in regard to the degree of aloofness from sensual pleasures and descending in regard to the degree of ascetic predilection. For instance, Mahāvīra's order was one degree removed from the Buddhist order in regard to ascetic practices, and the Ājivikas or Maskarins, one degree removed from the Jainas. Now looking the other way, the Brāhmaṇa Paribbājakas were one degree removed from the Buddhist in regard to their interest in worldly concerns associated with sensual pleasures, the Brahmin mahāsālas, one degree removed from the Brahmin Paribbājakas, the writers on statecraft (Arthakāras), one degree removed from the Dharmakāras, and so forth. This itself is a proof of the influence of the six Tirthikas upon the Buddhist order and of the influence of the orders of Mahāvīra's predecessors on his own. It enables us to make out the real significance of Buddha's famous declaration that he was a great reconciliator between the two extremes namely (1) the ideal of civic life, and (2) the ideal of asceticism.

In the account given in the Sāmaññaphala Sutta,

Mahāvīra is said to have laid great stress on the four-fold self-restraints (Cātuyāma Saṁvara); the term which is differently interpreted by Buddha first in relation to Mahāvīra, and secondly on his own account. In reference to Mahāvīra, the term is interpreted thus: "A Nigaṇṭha . . . . . lives restrained as regards all water; restrained as regards all evils; all evils he has washed away and he lives suffused with the sense of evil held at bay. Such is the four-fold self-restraint; and since he is thus tied with this four-fold bond, therefore is he the niggaṇṭho (free from bonds) called Gatatto (where heart is gone; that is to the summit, to the attainment of his aim), Ajatatto (whose heart is kept down; that is, is under command), and Thitatto (whose heart is fixed)."[1] Buddha explained the term somewhat differently when he explained it on his own account. By the four-fold self-restraint he meant the four moral precepts, each of which is viewed in its four-fold aspect.

In the Cūlasakuladāyi Sutta of the Majjhima Nikāya[2] we read that according to Mahāvīra, the four precepts and self-privation are the recognised roads to the blissful state of the soul. With regard to the first of the four restraints Buddhaghosa thought that the Jainas did not drink cold water on the ground that there were souls in it. The Jaina scruples about killing may be traced to the influence of Makkhali Gosāla, whose biological speculations gave rise to many religious problems, one of these being whether or not we were justified in taking life even for the purpose of food. We read in the Sūtrakritāṅga that the Hatthitāpasas were those who

[1] Sumaṅgala-Vilāsinī, pt. I, p. 168.

[2] Vol. II, pp. 35–36.

used to kill every year one elephant for the purpose of food, on the ground that thereby they minimised the slaughter of life.[1] The Brahmin law-givers prohibited the eating of certain kinds of fish and flesh. But the selection has nothing to do with a total prohibition of all kinds of fish and flesh enjoined by the religious feeling of the recluses. The Upālisutta of the Majjhima Nikāya[2] contains an interesting discussion of this subject. The Jaina householder Upāli pointed out that according to his master every act of killing is a cause of demerit whether the act be intentional or not. Buddha demurred to this view of Mahāvīra: he thought that a man commits no sin when the act is unintentional. It is impossible according to the Buddha to abstain from killing, for, even in moving about, a man is bound to put to death many lives. The Jainas took exception to the Buddhist view and an interesting account of it is given in Sūtrakritāṅga.[3]

In the Kassapasīhanāda Sutta (Dīgha, Vol. I) Buddha gives a general account of the Acelakas (naked ascetics).

The same acount is incorporated in the Aṅguttara Nikāya, Puggalapaññatti and other texts without any variation, which is a medley of laws and customs, that obtained amongst the various religious orders of the time, most of which were wearers of garments. This fragment can be compared with the Vaikhānasadharmasūtra also known as the Śrāmaṇakasūtra which is lost for ever, and which is frequently alluded to in the older Dharmasūtras now extant. In other words the Buddhist fragment is similar to the section of the Dharmasūtra

1 Jaina Sūtras, pt. II, p. 418. 2 Vol. I, p. 377.

3 Jain Sūtras, pt. II, pp. 414–417.

that professes to give a set of customary laws applicable to the Vānaprastha and Yati. The interest of the Buddhist passage lies in the fact that it invariably refers to the orders of the heretical teachers with whom we are concerned here. The Kesakamvalins were the wearers of blankets made up of hairs. As regards the Ājivika order founded by Nandavaccha, Kisasaṁkicca and Makkhali Gosāla, Buddha gives a separate account in the Mahāsaccaka Sutta of the Majjhima Nikāya (p. 238) which is really an abstract from the general account of the Acelakas mentioned above. The salient features of this account are given below.

The Ājivikas did not wear clothes. He cherished a very tender regard for all forms of life, and he developed a curious sense of freedom which led him not to obey another man's command. He was accustomed to fasting for days and weeks. In the Mahāsaccaka sutta (M.N.) a Jaina named Saccaka informed Buddha that the Ājivikas instead of leading such a moral life increased the strength and fat of their body by feeding on the best food and drink. In a passage of the Sūtrakritāṅga[1] a Jaina accuses Makkhali Gosālaputta of immoral habits, but Buddha's account prominently brings out the fact that the Ājivikas were far from being profligate and immoral. They were on the contrary advocates of the mode of the right living (Sammā ājivo) consistent with the principles of spiritual life, though the epithet 'Ājivikas' was used by the Jainas and Buddhists as a catchword for a person with household ties. From the meagre account given by Buddha and the Buddhist scriptures it is absolutely clear that the Ājivikas strictly

1 Jaina Sūtras, pt. II, p. 411.

observed as a rule almost all the moral precepts binding on the Jaina and the Buddhist order. Thus we can say that the idea of right living (Sammā ājivo) was taken by the Jainas and the Buddhists mainly from the Ājivikas. The influence of the so-called heretical teachers is not only prominent in matters of practice but also in their doctrine.

Let us examine this part of our subject without going into details. Let us first examine the doctrine of Pakudha Kaccāyana (Kukudha Kātyāyana). In the Jaina and the Buddhist works, his doctrine is designated differently ; the name signifies various aspects and phases :—

1. "Sassatavāda" (Brahmajāla-Sutta, Dīgha Nikāya, Vol. I, p. 1).

2. Aññājivo (the theory of duality) aññaṁsariravādo, Sattakāyavādo ātmashasṭavādo, anikyavādo.

3. Akiriyavādo.

The logical postulate of Kavandhin Kātyāyana's philosophy is nothing but the Parmenedian doctrine of Being. "Nothing comes out of nothing." (Noya uppajjae asaṁ). What is, does not perish ; from nothing comes nothing (sato nacci vinaso, asato nacci sambhavo). Sūtrakritāṅga (2. 1. 22). The Buddhist fragments do not make mention of this important logical principle. It is well known that this is the logical principle (Satkārya vāda) accepted in almost all the systems of Indian Philosophy, notably the system of the Bhagavat Gītā, the Sāṅkhya, the Vaiśeṣika, and the Vedānta. Among the earlier systems we might mention Jainism, Buddhism and the philosophy of the Upanishads, particularly that of Naciketā in Kathopanishat, which inculcates the same principle. These led the Jaina commentators Silāṅka and others to identify the doctrine of Pakudha with the system of the Bhagavat Gītā, the Sānkhāyam and some of the Shaiva systems. The ontological significance of its eternalism is summed up by Mahāvīra and Buddha in the expressions that the soul and the world (attā ca loko ca) are both eternal, giving birth to nothing new; that they are steadfast as a mountain peak, as a pillar firmly fixed. These principles are the same for ever and ever.

The epithet pluralism implies that Kaccāyana sought to explain the whole experience in the light of six or seven substances. The seven substances according to the Buddhist enumeration are earth, water, fire, air, pleasure, pain and soul. The six substances given by the Jainas are (1) earth, (2) water, (3) fire, (4) air, (5) space, and (6) soul.

The Jaina and the Buddhist accounts differ no doubt in some respects but they agree on the fundamental points.

We are led to understand that according to Kātyāyana the concrete existences are the results of the combination of the six or seven substances which perpetually unite and separate; unite by pleasure and separate by pain. Thus partly in agreement with Naciketā and partly in agreement with the Bhagavat Gītā, Kaccāyana aimed at explaining away birth and death as common phenomena in the world of experience.

The Pluralism of Kaccāyana is fitly summed up in the dualism of Pippalāda in the Prasnopanishat, that is, of Sāṅkhya.

Pippalāda, as it is well known, postulated prāṇa and rayi (that is, puruṣa and prakriti) the two ultimate principles relating to the explanation of all phenomena.

The logical consequence of his doctrine was fatal to

modern philosophy. If the substances are uncreated, uncaused, and eternally existent, and if they mechanically unite and disintegrate, the theory can ill afford to account for the moral distinction between good and bad, between right and wrong. This is the significance of the epithet akiriyavāda. Kaccāyana identified thought with being. The result was that he explained away the destinies of the particulars under the glamour of the universal concepts. Both Mahāvīra and Buddha rejected the position of Kaccāyana though theoretically they agreed with him that the real object of experience as a whole can never be cognised and described by appropriate symbols. Thus the influence exercised by Kaccāyana upon Jainism and Buddhism was rather of a negative character.

The way for Mahāvīra and Buddha was prepared by Ajitakesakambalī whose doctrine like that of Epicurus is generally misunderstood. The negative side of Ajita's philosophy is more prominent than its positive side. In its negative side his philosophy was employed to demolish the whole ground of the Brahmanic faith and ceremonial works. Indeed it breathed an utter contempt of everything Vedic or Brahmanic. He naively denied the possibility of re-birth and retribution. The world was just a concourse of four elements, the space being the repository of the senses, the soul being just a chemical product of matter and nothing more. Ajita rendered a great service to Indian Philosophy by the positive side of his philosophy which was directed against the dualistic or pluralistic theory of Kaccāyana. That which is psychical is corporal. ("Tam jīvo tam sariraṁ.") Thus Mahāvīra and Buddha fitly described the main content of Ajita's doctrine. What Ajita really contemplated was not to identify body with soul, or matter with spirit, but to point out that a particular object of experience must be somehow viewed as an indivisible whole.

Now the chieftain Pāyāsi who thought on the line of Ajita stated his predecessor's thesis in clear and unequivocal terms (Pāyāsi Suttanta, Dīgha Nikāya, Vol. II). In the language of the Sthānaṅga, such a doctrine is aptly designated "na santi paralokavādā." Mahāvīra and Buddha were right to suppose Ajita's doctrine of non-action (Akiriyavādā) because Ajita destroyed the ultimate ground of moral distinctions by denying the possibility of personal continuity and thus deprived life of its zest. However his services to Mahāvīra and Buddha were considerable. (1) He led them to think of reality or real object as a single indivisible whole, and (2) he led them to seek for the ground of moral distinctions in the volition of mind rather than anything else.

Pūraṇa Kassapa.—The Buddhist Sāmaññaphala Sutta gives a distorted and mutilated picture of the philosophical speculations of Pūraṇa Kassapa. The Buddhist teachers are led by their moral predilection to judge only of the moral bearing of Kassapa's philosophy. They assert that Pūraṇa Kassapa rules out the play of will in our moral life from the domain of speculation. The Jainas join hands with the Buddhists in grouping Kassapa's doctrine under Akiriyavāda. The Buddhist account keeps the theoretic side of Ajita's philosophy in the background. However, an important passage of the Jaina Sūtrakritāṅga[1] clearly states that his was really a theory of the passivity of soul. "When a

[1] Sūtrakritāṅga, i. i. 13.

man acts or causes another to act, it is not his soul which acts or causes to act (evaṁ akārayu appā)." The Jaina commentators identify this doctrine with Sāṅkhya philosophy which also posits the soul as a passive principle. In the absence of documents coming down to us from Kassapa, it is difficult even to imagine what was his conception of the part played by the soul in the conscious experience of the individual. The Sāṅkhya system speaks no doubt of the soul as a mere passive spectator while prakriti performs all active functions of the body and the mind. But he tried to get over the difficulty by asserting that the presence of the soul even as a passive spectator is essential to stir up energy in prakriti. Upadhi is the principle which connects body and mind with soul. Although such details of Kassapa's philosophy are unknown, it is undeniable that his theory of the passivity of the soul was an important step towards the development of the Sāṅkhya system from the rough outline given by Pippalāda. Thus we see that the influence of Pūraṇa Kassapa's speculation upon Jainism and Buddhism was rather of a negative character and the latter rejected in a body Kassapa's theory about the soul as absurd.

Makkhali Gosāla.—It is not improbable that by the theory of fortuitous origin or chance (adhiccasamuppādo, ahetuappaccayavādo, akāraṇavāda, yatdricchā in the Svetasvatara Upanishad) Buddha understood the logical postulate of the philosophy of Pūraṇa Kassapa besides that of the philosophy of the Vedas and Upanishads. Something comes into existence that was previously non-existent (ahutvā ahosi, that is to say, something comes out of nothing). This is the fundamental logical principle of Pūraṇa Kassapa as Buddha understood him. The term Adhiccasamuppāda is obviously the opposite of Buddha's paṭiccasamuppāda, the theory of causal genesis, which is explained thus: This is that comes to be, on the arising of this, that arises, etc. Of course, Pūraṇa Kassapa's principle was interpreted by Buddha from the moral standpoint, something comes out of nothing means that from the soul which is uncaused arises the experience of pleasure and pain, the sense of good and bad, etc. It is curious that the theory of non-causation or chance is ascribed to Makkhali Gosāla in the Sāmaññaphala Sutta, but the incompatibility of such a theory with the general trend of Gosāla's thought requires some explanation. The Aṅguttara Nikāya has a passage where the doctrine of Pūraṇa Kassapa and Makkhali Gosāla are mixed up by Ānanda. The interest of this passage is that the theory of chance is associated with the name of Pūraṇa Kassapa. Perhaps this confusion led Buddha Gautama to declare Gosāla's doctrine to be the worst of all. Mrs. Rhys Davids points out that in this passage Buddha confounded Gosāla with Ajitakesakambalī when he said in jest that the blanket made up of hair was hot in hot weather and cold in cold weather. Judging from the line of thought followed by Makkhali Gosāla, it seems that he was a fatalist or determinist rather than a propounder of the doctrine of chance. Everything was unalterably fixed. This was the fundamental thesis of Makkhali Gosāla as we read it in the Jaina Bhagavatī. Buddhaghosa also says that according to Gosāla, things happen exactly as they are to happen, that which is not to happen does not happen.[1] It is clear from this that

---

[1] Sumaṅgala-Vilāsinī, pp. 160–165.

Gosāla maintains that everything happens according to the unalterable laws of nature, that is to say, he banishes chance from the whole of experience. He seeks to explain things as a biologist in the light of these three principles : (1) Fate, (2) Species, and (3) Nature.

The pleasure and pain which living beings experience depend partly upon past deeds and partly upon their birth and inherent nature. (Niyatisaṅgatibhāvapariṇatā, Sāmaññaphala Sutta, Sūtrakritāṅga). Gosāla's is a theory of evolution of individual things by natural transformation (parināma implied in parinato). The Sāmaññaphala Sutta states his main thesis rather narrowly when it says that fools and wise alike wandering in transmigration make an end of pain (Sandhāvitvā saṁsaritvā dukkhassantaṁ karissanti). His doctrine is that all forms of life, all living substances, attain perfection after having gradually passed higher and higher through different types of existence which are fixed, and after having experienced pleasure and pain, peculiar to each form of existence. The highest in the scale of existence is of course a Jīna (perfect man). Now his theory of evolution differs fundamentally from Darwin's theory as it implies an evolution not of species but of individuals, from a lower species to a higher one. In working out his theory of perfection by transformation Gosāla classifies the living things in various ways and arranges them in an ascending order and he seems to give a two-fold classification, psychological and physiological. But it is implied in his view that organic development progresses side by side with the development of mind. He conceives infinity of time, involving a conception of kalpas (cycles), antarakalpas, meaning uniform succession of the cycles of existence; but time for individual is finite or limited in both ways as illustrated by the simile of a ball of string which spreads out just as far and no further than it can unwind. For Gosāla there is not only a gradation of the types of existence, but also there are eight stages of development in the life of a man, at each of which the mental growth corresponds to the physical and vice versa. The theory of the gradual development connects Gosāla with the past, the Aitareyas in particular (Aitareya Āraṇyaka), and with succeeding ages, which had seen the birth of the religious philosophies of Mahāvīra and Buddha. Gosāla's biological speculations supply his worthy successors with ample food for thought, with arguments which are put by them mainly to a moral, social and, in short, to a practical use. One illustration will suffice. In the Vāseṭṭha Sutta of the Suttanipāta, Buddha opposes the caste system on grounds drawn from biology. The theory of caste or yāti is untenable as it introduces species within species. Buddha gives a list of species of various animals, insects and plants and holds that such a variety of species is not to be found among men (Suttanipāta, p. 115, verse 14). The theory of caste or yāti easily breaks down when we see that a Brahmin and a caṇḍāla do not differ in their physical constitution and can together procreate children.

A short and malicious fragment in the Sāmaññaphala Sutta tells us that Gosāla divides actions into act, word and thought: thought being regarded as half karma. This division of karma which some writers suppose to be derived from the Zendāvestā was really an indigenous growth in India and played an important part in the Jaina and Buddhist thought. As a naturalist, Gosāla lays stress on act and word; Buddha as a psychologist lays stress on thought or volition (cetanā); Mahāvīra who forms a connecting link between them is said to have laid equal stress on manokamma and kāyakamma on the ground of the interaction of body and mind (Cittanvayo kāyo hoti, kāyanvayaṁ cittaṁ hoti).[1] The deterministic theory of Makkhali Gosāla constitutes a moral difficulty. If living beings are bent this way and that way by their fate, how can we make them responsible for their actions? Both Mahāvīra and Buddha think that Makkhali's theory leaves no room for the freedom of the will. That is to say, his is a doctrine of non-action (akiriyavādo). But in point of fact the moral freedom of men is not inconsistent with the deterministic theory of Gosāla and the relation of Gosāla's theory to Indian philosophy in general and to moral philosophy in particular is that it establishes the governance of law in the universe of experience. It also tacitly suggests that not only physical phenomena but also mental and moral phenomena are subject to definite laws. Thus we see that he gives his successors caution, that moral freedom, if there be any, must be freedom of being within the operation of laws. If will is to be operative, it must operate in accordance with the general order of things.

Sañjaya Belaṭṭhiputto.—It is still an open question whether Sañjaya Belaṭṭhiputto was the same person as Sañjaya, the wanderer, the former teacher of Sāriputta, who became later on the chief disciple of Buddha. Prof. Jacobi has identified the two names.[2] Of course the Belaṭṭhiputto himself was a far-famed wandering teach-

---

1 Majjhima Nikāya, Vol. I, p. 238.

2 Jaina Sūtras, pt. II, p. xxix.

er of the time. There is mention of a Sañjaya in the Jaina Uttarādhyayana Sūtra.[1] There it is stated that he was converted to the Jaina faith by Gardhavāli. Supposing that Belaṭṭhiputto was no other than the wanderer and that Sāriputta was the connecting link between him and the Buddha, we can show how scepticism as a philosophic method was superseded in course of time by a method which was critical. The transition did not however take place abruptly. Sañjaya's contribution to Indian philosophy was similar to that of Pyrrho in Greek philosophy, who visited India and studied philosophy under the Gymnosophists in the 4th century B.C. His contribution was a negative or destructive one, as it aimed at avoiding all dogmatic conclusions. He was the first to maintain a neutral attitude towards the dogmatic views of life and things and to prove that it was impossible to offer certitude for human knowledge concerning the reality of life and things. He was the first to turn men's attention away from vain speculations and to teach that the best pathway to peace lay elsewhere, in preserving a tranquil state of mind. Thus he suggested the problems to be excluded from the domain of speculation and he inaugurated a critical era dominated by higher ethical ideals.

As a philosopher, Sañjaya belonged to the sophistic period and his doctrine was unintelligible except in relation to the teachings of Pakudha Kaccāyana and Ajita Kesakambalī.

---

[1] Jaina Sūtras, pt. II, p. 82.

CHAPTER IV.

BUDDHAGHOSA'S COMMENTARIES.

Tradition ascribes to Thera Buddhaghosa the authorship of several exegetical works, which, as we have them now, are headed by the encyclopaedic Visuddhimagga. He is said to have written commentaries on the whole of the Vinaya Piṭaka including the Pātimokkha, the four Nikāyas, and on the seven books of the Abhidhamma-Piṭaka. The commentaries on some of the important books of the Khuddaka Nikāya are also attributed to him. Regarding Buddhaghosa, Mrs. Rhys Davids says, "It may readily be granted that Buddhaghosa must not be accepted *en bloc.* The distance between the constructive genius of Gotama and his apostles as compared with the succeeding ages of epigoni needs no depreciatory criticism on the labours of the exegesists to make itself felt forcibly enough. Buddhaghosa's philology is doubtless crude and he is apt to leave the cruces unexplained, concerning which an Occidental is most in the dark. Nevertheless, to me his work is not only highly suggestive, but also a mine of historic interest. To put it aside is to lose the historical perspective of the course of Buddhist Philosophy."[1]

Here, however, we are concerned with the works of Buddhaghosa as revealing the development of his own mind rather than bringing out the expositions of his earlier thoughts.

---

[1] Introductory Essay, Buddhist Psychological Ethics, p. xxv.

Origin and Development of Commentaries.

Before we discuss the question of the origin and development of Buddhaghosa's commentaries, a word or two about the nature of a commentary seems necessary. A commentary means reading new meanings back into old texts according to one's own education and outlook. Its motive is to explain the words and judgments of others as accurately and faithfully as possible. This remark applies equally to all commentaries, Sanskrit and Pāli alike.

The teacher Revata is represented as saying to his pupil Buddhaghosa, "The Pāli or Tripiṭaka only has been brought over here, no commentary is extant in this place. The divergent opinions of teachers other than the Theravādins do not likewise exist. The Ceylon commentary, which is free from faults, and which was written in Sinhalese by thoughtful Mahinda with due regard to the methods of expositions, taught by the Supreme Buddha, put up before the three councils, and rehearsed by Sāriputta and others, is current among the people of Ceylon. Please go there and study it and then translate it into Māgadhi which will be useful to the whole world." [1]

From this it is evident that the commentaries were not to be found in India at the time of Buddhaghosa; they were all to be found in Ceylon. It follows further that the commentaries, as they come down to us, were not the original compositions of either Buddhaghosa or his illustrious predecessor Mahinda. These commentaries, as it appears from tradition, were originally the productions not of a single author but of a community

[1] Mahāvaṁsa, Ch. 7, Anderson's Pāli Reader, p. 28.

of monks. Mahinda was merely a translator in Sinhalese and Buddhaghosa a retranslator in Pāli.

Buddhaghosa himself freely admits in his prologues to several commentaries,[1] that he annotated those passages only which were not commented upon by his predecessors, and the rest he only translated. All available evidence points to the fact that within the first decade of Buddha's enlightenment, Buddhist headquarters were established in various localities adjoining many important towns and cities of the time, viz. Benares, Rājagaha, Vesālī, Nālandā, Pāvā, Ujjenī, Campā, Madhurā, Ulumpā, and so on. At every one of these places sprang up a community of Bhikkhus under the leadership and guidance of a famous disciple of the Buddha such as Mahākassapa, Mahākaccāyana, Mahākoṭṭhita, Sāriputta, Moggallāna, and the like. Following the rule of the wanderers or sophists they used to spend the rainy season in a royal pleasure garden or a monastery, after which they generally met together once a year at Rājagaha, Beluvana, Sāvatthī or elsewhere. Friendly interviews among themselves, and occasional calls on contemporary sophists, were not unknown. Among these various leaders of Bhikkhus, some ranked foremost in doctrine, some in discipline, some in ascetic practices, some in story-telling, some in analytical expositions, some in preaching, some in philosophy, some in poetry, and so on.[2] Among Buddha's disciples and followers there were men who came of Brāhmin families, and who mastered the Vedas and the whole of Vedic literature. It may be

---

[1] Sumaṅgala-Vilāsinī I, p. 1 (P.T.S.). Sāratthapakāsinī, p. 1.

[2] *Vide* Etadaggavaggo, Aṅguttara Nikāya I; Mahāvaṁsa, edited by Geiger, 'The Council of Mahākassapa.'

naturally asked: What were these profoundly learned and thoughtful Bhikkhus doing all the time?

The Buddhist and Jaina texts tell us that the itinerant teachers of the time wandered about in the country, engaging themselves wherever they stopped in serious discussions on matters relating to religion, philosophy, ethics, morals and polity.[1] Discussions about the interpretation of the abstruse utterances of the great teacher were frequent and the *raison d'être* of the developments of the Buddhist literature, particularly of the commentaries, is to be traced in these discussions. There are numerous interesting passages in the Tripiṭaka, telling us how from time to time contemporary events suggested manifold topics of discussion among the Bhikkhus, or how their peace was disturbed by grave doubts calling forth explanations either from the Buddha himself or from his disciples. Whenever some interested sophists spoke vehemently 'in many ways in dispraise of the Buddha, the Doctrine and the Order,'[2] whenever another such sophist misinterpreted Buddha's opinion,[3] whenever a furious discussion broke out in any contemporary Brotherhood,[4] or whenever a Bhikkhu behaved improperly, the Bhikkhus generally assembled under the pavilion to discuss the subject, or were exhorted by Buddha or by his disciples to safeguard their interests. It was on one such occasion that Buddha was led to offer an historical exposition of the moral precepts

---

1 *Vide* my paper "A short account of the wandering teachers at the time of the Buddha" (J.A.S.B.) New series, Vol. XVI, No. 7, 1918.

2 Dīgha-Nikāya, I, p. 2.

3 Majjhima-Nikāya, III, pp. 207–8.

4 Ibid., Sāmagāmasutta, II, pp. 243–4.

in accordance with his famous doctrine. "One should avoid all that is evil, and perform all that is good"[1] that is to say, an explanation of the precepts in their negative and positive aspects. This is now incorporated in the first thirteen suttas of the Dīgha-Nikāya, and is familiarly known as the Sīlakkhanda,—"The tract on morality,"—lending its name to the first volume of the Dīgha.[2] On another occasion Potaliputta, the wanderer, called on Samiddhi, and informed him thus: "According to Samaṇa Gotama, as I actually heard him saying, Kamma either by way of deed or by way of word is no Kamma at all, the real Kamma being by way of thought or volition only. For there is an attainment after having reached which, one feels nothing (i.e. which transcends all sensible experience and pleasure and pain)."

"Speak not, friend Potaliputta, thus, speak not of him in this manner. Please do not misrepresent our teacher's point of view, for that is not good. He would never have said so."

"But tell me, friend Samiddhi, what a man will experience as the consequence of his deliberate action by way of thought, word and deed." "Pain," was the reply.[3]

When a report of this discussion was submitted to Buddha, he regretted that the muddle-headed Samiddhi had given such a one-sided answer to the second point of the wanderer whom he had never met in his life. For the right and complete answer would in that case

---

1 "Sabba pāpassa akaranam, kusalassa upasampadā."

2 "The Dialogues of the Buddha," S.B.B., Vol. II, pp. 3–26.

3 The rendering is not literal, though substantially faithful.

have been that 'he will experience either pleasure or pain or neither pleasure nor pain.' But as regards Samiddhi's reply to the first point, he had nothing to say against it.

Be that as it may, the fact remains that the wisdom and folly of Samiddhi, yet a junior learner, formed the argument of Buddha's longer analytical exposition of the all-important subject of Kamma, which he termed the Mahākammavibhaṅga [1] in contradistinction to his shorter exposition, the Cūlakammavibhaṅga, [2] which was addressed to a young Brahmin scholar named Subha. Thus it can be established that the Mahākammavibhaṅga was the Sutta basis of the Abhidhamma exposition of the Sikkhāpadavibhaṅga which is incorporated in the second book of the Abhidhamma Piṭaka.[3] But as a matter of fact, both these expositions have left their stamp on subsequent exegetical literature as is evidenced by the Nettipakaraṇa and the Atthasālinī and other such works. Scanning the matter closely we can say that Buddhaghosa's exposition of kamma in his Atthasālinī is really the meeting place of both.

The Majjhima Nikāya contains many other illuminating expositions of Buddha, notably the Saḷāyataṇa Vibhaṅga,[4] the Araṇavibhaṅga,[5] the Dhātu Vibhaṅga,[6] and the Dakkhinā Vibhaṅga,[7] which have found their due places in the Abhidhamma literature,[8] supplemented by higher expositions. They also have found their way

---

1 Majjhima-Nikāya, III, pp. 207–215.

2 Ibid., III, pp. 202–206. Nettipakaraṇa, pp. 182–183.

3 Vibhaṅga, pp. 285–291.

4 Majjhima Nikāya, Vol. III, pp. 215–222.

5 Ibid., pp. 230–237.

6 Ibid., pp. 237–247.

7 Ibid., pp. 253–257.

8 Vibhaṅga, pp. 70–73; 82–90. Cf. Dhātukathā, etc.

into the later commentaries including, of course, the monumental works of Thera Buddhaghosa. Then we have from Thera Sāriputta, the chief disciple of Buddha, a body of expositions of the four Aryan truths, the Saccavibhaṅga [1] or Saccaniddesa,[2] which has found its due place in the second book of the Abhidhamma Piṭaka, where it has been supplemented by a higher exposition (Abhidhammabhājaniya) based upon the sutta exposition.[3] Sāriputta's exposition contains many of these stock passages or the older disconnected materials with which the whole of the Piṭaka literature, as we may reasonably suppose, was built up. This piece of independent commentary has been tacked on to the Satipaṭṭhāna Sutta, itself a commentary, and furnishes a datum of distinction between the Satipaṭṭhāna Sutta in the Majjhima Nikāya and the Mahāsatipaṭṭhāna Sutta in the Dīgha Nikāya.

A complete catechism of important terms and passages of exegetical nature is ascribed to Sāriputta and is familiarly known as the Mahā Saṅgīti Suttanta,[4] of which a Buddhist Sanskrit version exists in Tibetan and Chinese translations under the name of Sangīti Parayāya Sūtra. The method of grouping various topics under numerical heads and of explaining by means of simple enumeration, invariably followed by Thera Sāriputta in the singularly interesting catechism above referred to, characterises two of the older connections, the Saṁyutta and Aṅguttara and certain books of the Abhidhamma

---

1 Majjhima Nikāya, III, pp. 248–252.

2 Mahāsatipaṭṭhāna Suttanta, Dīgha Nikāya.

3 Vibhaṅga, pp. 193–205.

4 Dīgha Nikāya, III, See for references Prof. Tākākusu's highly instructive article on the Sarvāstivādins in J.P.T.S., 1905, p. 67.

Piṭaka, notably the Puggala Paññatti, the materials of which were mostly drawn from the Aṅguttara Nikāya. This is a fact which alone can bring home to us the nature of Sāriputta's work in connection with the Piṭaka literature. But Sāriputta does not exhaust the list. We have to consider other renowned and profoundly learned disciples of Buddha, among whom some were women, who in their own way helped forward the process of development of the commentaries. Take, for example, the case of the Thera Mahākaccāyana who was allowed to enjoy the reputation of one who could give a detailed exposition of what was said by Buddha in brief.[1] The Majjhima Nikāya alone furnishes four exegetical fragments[2] written by Mahākaccāyana, which are of great value as forming the historical basis of the three later works,[3] two in Pāli and one in Buddhist Sanskrit, which are all ascribed to him. The few fragments by Mahākaccāno (Mahakaccāyana) which have reached us are important for another reason: they exhibit the working of the human mind in different directions. It is interesting to note that Mahākaccāno, so far as we can judge from these older fragments, seldom indulges in mechanical enumeration and in the coining of technical terms as Sāriputta did. He, on the contrary, confines himself to bringing out the inner significance and true philosophical bearing of Buddha's first principles.

Then we have to make our acquaintance with Thera Mahakoṭṭhita who was an authority next to none but Buddha himself on Paṭisambhidā or methodology of

---

1 Dīpavaṁsa (Oldenberg), p. 109.

2 Majjhima Nikāya, I, pp. 110 foll.; III, pp. 78, 194, 223.

3 Viz., Nettipakaraṇa, Peṭakopadesa, Jñānaprasthāna Śāstra.

Buddha's analytical system. He gives us the characteristic marks or specific differences of current abstract terms signifying the various elements of experience.[1] He warns us at the same time against a possible misconception. Reason, understanding, perception, sensation and so forth are not entities. They are not dissociated, but all are inseparably associated[2] in reality. The first part of Mahākoṭṭhita's explanation may be said to be the historical foundation of the Lakkhaṇahāra in the Nettipakaraṇa, of some passages in the Milinda-Pañho,[3] in the commentaries[4] of Buddhaghosa ; we have similar contributions from Moggallāna, Ānanda, Dhammadinnā and Khemā, but we need not multiply instances.

A careful examination of the contents of the second book of the Abhidhamma Piṭaka has proved beyond doubt that there is no hard and fast line between the Sutta and the Abhidhamma Piṭakas, the division resting mainly upon a difference of *modus operandi*. The Abhidhamma method was based upon and followed closely in the line of the Sutta exposition which is evidently earlier. It goes without saying that the difference between the two methods is not only one of degree but at times one of kind. In spite of the fact that the Abhidhamma exposition is direct, definite and methodical, we cannot say that in all cases its value is greater than the Sutta exposition. There will always be a difference of opinion among Buddhist scholars as to whether

---

1 Pajānāti pajānātītī .... tasmā paññavā ti vuccati ....
Vijānāti vijānātīti .... tasmā viññananti vuccati ....
Majjhima Nikāya, I, p. 292.

2 Ibid., Ime dhammā saṃsaṭṭhā no visaṃsaṭṭhā.....

3 Milinda-Pañho, p. 62. (Edited by Trenckner.)

4 e.g. Sumaṅgala-Vilāsinī, I, pp. 62–65.

the Adhidhamma books contain the genuine words of Buddha Gotama.[1] It is nevertheless certain that the major part of that literature is based upon the teachings and expositions of the great teacher.

There may be a Sariputta or some other unseen hands at work behind the scene, but, on the whole, the credit, as history proves it, belongs ultimately to Buddha himself. The whole of the Abhidhamma Piṭaka has been separately classed by Buddhaghosa as Veyyākaraṇa or Exposition. We are told that this class comprises also the gāthāless or prose suttas which are not found in the remaining eight classes of early Buddhist literature.[2] The foregoing discussion has shown that the Vedallas need not be grouped as a separate class. There is no reason why the Cūlavedalla and the Mahāvedalla suttas in the Majjhima Nikāya should not be included in the veyyākaraṇa class. At all events it has been clearly proved that in the Tripiṭakas, excluding the Kathāvatthu, which was composed in the 3rd century B.C., we have two layers, so to say, of Veyyākaraṇa, viz. the Suttabhājanīya and the Abhidhammabhājanīya Khandha, Vibhaṅga, Niddesa—these are but different synonyms of the same term. That is to say, the suttas containing terminology, definition, enumeration or explanation, whether with or without such names as Khandha, Vibhaṅga, Niddesa, constitute the first great landmark; and the six Abhidhamma books, largely based upon the suttas, the second landmark in the history of Buddhist commentaries. The third landmark is not easy to determine. Here we have a choice between a

1 See for a learned discussion on the subject among the Theras-Atthasālinī, pp. 29–31.

2 Sumaṅgala-Vilāsinī (Burmese edition), p. 324, Atthasālinī, p. 26.

few works [1] ascribed to Mahākaccāno and the Kathāvatthu of which Thera Moggaliputta Tissa is said to be the author. As regards the date of the latter, it is almost certain that the book was composed about the time of the third Buddhist council held under the auspices of King Aśoka. The case of Mahākaccāno's works is somewhat different. A careful survey of the Peṭakopadesa which is still buried in manuscripts shows that whatever might be its date of composition, it is a supplementary treatise to the Nettipakaraṇa of which a beautiful edition in Roman character is given to us by Prof. E. Hardy. A Buddhist Sanskrit work, the Jñānaprasthāna Śāstra by a Mahākātyāyana, is held, as Prof. Tākākusu informs us, as an authoritative text by the Sarvāstivādins. This Śāstra is mentioned by Vasuvandhu in his Abhidharmakoṣa [2] as one of the seven Abhidhamma books. The work was translated into Chinese by Saṅghadeva and another in A.D. 383. Another translation was made in A.D. 657 by Hiuen Tsang who translated also the Abhidharmamahāvibhāsaśāstra, a commentary on Mahākātyāyana's work composed during the council under Kaniṣka.[3] The Chinese traveller tells us that the Jñānaprasthāna śāstra was composed three hundred years after the death of Buddha. Buddhist scholars have yet to settle the question whether or not Jñānaprasthāna has anything in common with the Nettipakaraṇa or with Paṭṭhāna, the seventh book of the Abhidhamma Piṭaka. The Netti, as we now have it, contains a section named Sāsanapaṭṭhāna which embodies a classification of the Piṭaka passages according

---

1 Hardy, Introduction to the Nettipakaraṇa, p. xxxii f. n. 1.

2 E. Burnouf's Introduction, p. 447.

3 Beal Buddhist Records, I, pp. 174–175.

to their leading thoughts. Judging from the valuable extracts from the Jñānaprasthāna given by Prof. Tākākusu, we can decide once for all that the work is not identical with the Pāli Abhidhamma book, Paṭṭhāna, though presumably it bears some resemblance to the latter. The Netti and Jñānaprasthāna have many points in common, as they were written to serve a similar purpose.

In the opening paragraphs or pages of his two books, Mahākaccāyana frankly states that his work was not to start a new idea but to produce a systematic and analytical exposition of the expressions of others (paratoghosā).[1] The Parikkhārahāra[2] of the Netti is a chapter based upon the paṭṭhāna, though it throws new light on the subject of causal correlation. As appears from the section on Nayasamuṭṭhāna, Mahākaccāyana refers to the Buddhist schismatics or heretics (Diṭṭhicaritā asmiṁ sāsane pabbajitā), whom he sharply distinguished from the outsiders (Diṭṭhicaritā bahiddhāpabbajitā). Such a thing as this is not possible within the first century of Buddha's Nibbāṇa. It presupposes the four Nikāyas and all other older books of the three Piṭakas from which it has quoted several passages. Without going into further details, we shall not be far from the truth to suppose that the works of Mahākaccāyana were indeed a connecting link between the Tripiṭaka on one side and all subsequent Buddhist texts on the other. Thus if we have to choose between his works and the Kathāvatthu, the priority must be said to belong to the former.

---

1 B. M. Barua's Prolegomena to a history of Buddhist Philosophy, pp. 10, 42.

2 Nettipakaraṇa, pp. 78–80.

The Kathāvatthu, which is a Buddhist book of debate on matters of theology and philosophy, represents the fourth landmark. Buddhaghosa's [1] plea for affiliation of this significant text to the Pāli canon is ingenious enough. Buddha laid down the main propositions (Mātikā) which were discussed later by the adherents of different schools of thought.[2] It may, however, be doubted whether a book of controversy such as the Kathāvatthu can be regarded as a landmark in the history of the commentaries. But a closer investigation will make it evident that this book of controversy is looked upon in one way as no more than a book of interpretation, as Mahākaccāyana [3] rightly points out that the Buddhist heretics, in spite of their individual differences, agreed so far as their regard for the teachings of the master was concerned. The few specimens of controversy which the Kathāvatthu has embodied show that both sides referred to Buddha as a final court of appeal. All have quoted passages from the canon, though their interpretations differ widely. Next we have to think of the "Questions of King Milinda" (Milinda-Pañho) which is a romantic dialogue between King Menander and Thera Nāgasena. It presupposes the Kathāvatthu and may be regarded philosophically as a richer synthesis of the isolated movements of Buddhist thought than the former.[4]

The time when the Milinda-Pañho was composed and when Buddhaghosa was writing out his own works,

---

[1] Nettipakaraṇa, pp. 110-112.

[2] Atthasālinī, pp. 4–6.

[3] Nettipakaraṇa, p. 122.

[4] Kathāvatthu Commentary by Buddhaghosa; Vasumitra's work on the 18 schools.

quoting various Sinhalese commentaries,[1] can be pointed out as the sixth landmark. Besides these Ceylon commentaries, Buddhaghosa has made casual reference to the opinions of the Dīghabhānakas,[2] the Majjhimabhānakas [3] and other such schools of Theras. In his introduction to the Sumaṅgala-Vilāsinī [4] he gives us a short account of these schools of Theras which were originally but so many schools of recitation rather than of opinion. In the background of Buddhaghosa's works which are catalogued here as the seventh landmark, there are the whole of Tripiṭaka, the works of Mahākaccāyana, the Kathāvatthu, the Milinda-Pañho, the Pannattivāda of teachers other than the Theravādins, certain Vitaṇḍāvādins, Pakativāda [5] (the Sāṅkhya or the Yoga system), and the views of Bhikkhus [6] of Ceylon. To sum up: there is evidence enough to confirm the truth of the tradition that neither Buddhaghossa, nor Thera Mahinda, nor the Theras of old, were the originators of the commentaries; but we cannot agree with them when they all deny their claim to originality. The Niddesa which is an old commentary on certain suttas in the Sutta Nipāta cannot compare favourably with Buddhaghosa's Paramatthajotikā. The Peṭakopadesa [7] of Mahākaccāyana, of which a passage is quoted by Buddhaghosa, is not the Atthasālinī. In justice to all, we can say that Buddha himself, his disciples and their disciples were those who prepared the way for great Buddhaghosa, the commentator.

---

[1] Buddhist Manual of Psychological Ethics, pp. xxiii–xxiv.

[2] and [3] Atthasālinī, pp. 151, 399, 407, 420. [4] pp. 11–15.

[5] Atthasālinī (Sinhalese Edition), pp. 3, 90, 92, 241.

[6] Puggala-Paññatti Commentary (Sinhalese Edition), p. 722.

[7] Atthasālinī, p. 165. Peṭake vuttaṁ.

Enquiries into Buddhaghosa's Commentaries.

A critical survey of Buddhaghosa's works suggests to an inquiring mind many far-reaching questions of which very few have indeed been hitherto examined or answered. Perhaps the most important of them is this:—How far has Buddhaghosa revealed himself in his commentaries headed by the Visuddhimagga? In other words, what historical information about Buddhaghosa's life can be culled from his works? Other questions that may arise are all subsidiary to this. We may ask, for example, (1) Supposing, as the Mahāvaṁsa would have us believe, that Buddhaghosa was born in a Brahmin family of Gayā, mastered the Vedic literature with all its auxiliary sciences and arts and learnt the views of Patañjali so well that he could cite them verbatim, it is to be inquired: can we find any trace of the influence of Brahmanic culture and of the system of Patañjali on his works? (2) Where did he meet Thera Revata, who converted him to the Buddhist faith after defeating him by means of arguments in a philosophical discussion? (3) Can we give any substantial proof in support of the tradition that he wrote his Atthasālinī while in India? (4) What reminiscences of Ceylon are to be found in his commentaries? (5) What light is thrown by his works on the social, political, philosophical, literary, and artistic history of India of his time? (6) What is the relation of Buddhaghosa to Buddhadatta and other teachers of South India in regard to the interpretation of Buddhist philosophy? (7) What are his social contributions to Buddhist or to Indian philosophy? (8) In what way was Buddhaghosa a connecting link between Northern India, the Deccan and Ceylon? (9) Can we discover in Buddhaghosa any anticipation of Saṅkara?

(10) What is the place of Buddhaghosa as a writer and philosopher in the history of India, particularly in the history of Buddhism? (11) How is it that Buddhaghosa makes no reference to Mahāyāna Buddhism? (12) What is the immediate background of Buddhaghosa's philosophy? (13) What is the extent of the indebtedness of Buddhaghosa to the Buddhist kings and teachers of Ceylon? As each of these questions requires a separate paper, we shall content ourselves in the following pages with attempting to answer only one with the help of the available records.

Buddhaghosa in his Commentaries.

Buddhaghosa has left for us no other record of his life than his commentaries. The information that comes from other sources is meagre. Mr. Gray was the first to collect in his Buddhaghosuppatti some references to his life from the Mahāvaṁsa, the Sāsanavaṁsa, and the like. The accounts given in these works are hardly anything but anecdotes which may be summed up as follows :—

Buddhaghosa was born in a Brahmin family in the vicinity of the Bodhi terrace. He was brought up during his early years in Brahmanic tradition. He mastered the three Vedas together with all the supplementary works on science and art. He was an adherent of the system of Patañjali previous to his adoption of the Buddhist faith. Following the usage of his time he wandered about in the country as a sophist. He called at a monastery where he happened to meet a Thera Revata who is said to have defeated him in a philosophical discussion. He studied the Pāli Tripiṭaka under Revata. He wrote a philosophical treatise entitled the

Ñanodaya. He also wrote a commentary on a certain section of the Dhammasaṅgaṇi under the name of the Atthasālinī. He was engaged in writing a Parittaaṭṭhakathā when Thera Revata urged him to go to Ceylon. The Sāsanavaṁsa tells us that he accidentally met on the way Thera Buddhadatta who was then returning from Ceylon.[1]

Buddhaghosa visited Ceylon during the reign of King Mahānāma; the sole object of his journey to Ceylon was to retranslate the Sinhalese commentaries into Māgadhi. He studied the Sinhalese commentaries under Thera Saṅghapāla of Mahāvihāra at Anurādhapura. There he produced the Visuddhimagga which is esteemed as an encyclopaedia of Buddhism. After that he spent his time at the Ganthakāra Monastery where he composed all his commentaries; thereafter he returned to India. It is recorded in the Sāsanavaṁsa that Buddhaghosa was a native of Ghosagāma near the Bodhi terrace. The Brahmin Kesī was his father and Kesiyā his mother. The primary object of his voyage to Ceylon was to retranslate the Tripiṭaka into Pāli. The Mahavaṁsa is silent on these details.

Buddhaghosa is reticent about himself. He nowhere tells us who he was or where he was born. There are occasional references to Ceylon and to his teachers and friends, from which nothing definite can be inferred regarding his own life. That the Visuddhimagga was his first production in Ceylon is beyond dispute. In the preface to his Samantapāsādikā, the commentary on the Vinaya Piṭaka, he tells us that this was the first commentary on the canonical texts. He makes an apology

---

[1] Sāsanavaṁsa, p. 29.

for undertaking to write a commentary on the Vinaya Piṭaka first, contrary to the usual order of Dhamma and Vinaya. He says that Vinaya is the foundation of the Buddhist faith. The Samantapāsādikā was followed by his commentaries on the four Nikāyas in succession, which preceded his commentaries on the seven books of the Abhidhamma Piṭaka. The Jātaka commentary was evidently composed before the Paramatthajotikā being a serial commentary on certain books of the Khuddaka-nikāya. His later commentaries refer to his earlier ones [1] and all presuppose his Visuddhimagga.[2] Hence a concordance of them may be an invaluable aid to the study of Buddhaghosa and his works.

Buddhaghosa was an inhabitant of south Behār. This part of the tradition may be taken for granted. His connection with the Brahmin family and with Brahmanic tradition is undeniable. The evidence of his commentaries amply bears this out. His comment upon the Pāli passage [3] relative to the supplementary treatises of the Vedas could not be expected from one who was not conversant with the whole of the Vedic literature. His emphasis on Vinaya is another proof of the influence of his previous learning. His definitions of killing, theft, etc., show an enormous improvement on older exposi-

---

[1] Sumaṅgala-Vilāsinī, I, p. 70. "Atthikehi Samantapāsādikaṁ Vinayaṭṭhakathaṁ oloketvā gahetabaṁ." Puggala-Paññatti Commentary, p. 222. "Ayaṁ Aṅgnttaraṭṭhakathaṁ nayo." Atthasālinī refers to the Samantapāsādikā, pp. 97, 98. Vibhaṅga Commentary, p. 407.

[2] Atthasālinī, pp. 168, 183, 186, 187, 190, 198. Sumaṅgalavilāsinī, p. 2. Puggala-paññatti, p. 254.

[3] Sumaṅgalavilāsinī, I, p. 248. "Mahāpurisalakkhanaṁti mahāpurisānaṁ Buddhādinaṁ lakkhaṇa-dīpakaṁ dvādasasahassagandhappamānaṁ satthaṁ."

tions. Buddha as a psychologist was quite content with the definition of Kamma as volition (Cetanā Bhikkave vadāmi Kammaṁ). Buddhaghosa framed a definition accordingly.[1] But, as appears from his explanation, for him an action is no action until the will is actually manifested in conduct,[2] which goes to prove that his point of view was juristic or practical.

The tradition telling us that he was an adherent of the system of Patañjali also seems to have historical accuracy. He is insolent throughout his works in his attacks on Pakativāda, i.e., the Sāṅkhya or the Yoga system. He shows extravagant zeal for differentiating the Buddhist conception of Avijjā from the Pakativādin's conception of Pakati as the root cause of things,[3] and the Buddhist conception of Nāmarūpa from the outsider's conception of Puruṣa and Prakriti. He betrays nevertheless his previous relation with the Sāṅkhya and the Yoga systems. His conception of Nāmarūpa is very much like the Sāṅkhya conception of Puruṣa and Prakriti. Even the very simile of the blind and the lame by which the two conceptions are illustrated is the same.[4] It might be argued that Buddhaghosa based his conception on the authority of the earlier Buddhist thinkers, notably Nāgasena and Asvaghoṣa.[5] But who can deny that the Buddhist thinkers, too, were greatly influenced by the Sāṅkhya line of thinking ? Indeed taking into consideration all available evidence, we cannot but

---

1 Sumaṅgalavilāsinī, pt. I, p, 69.

2 Cf. Sumaṅgalavilāsinī.

3 Visuddhimagga (Sinhalese Edition), pp. 407–408.

4 Cf. the passage in Vyāsa's Commentary on Yoga Sūtra III, 44. Atthasālinī, p. 61.

5 Paramatthajotikā II, p. 169.

agree with M. Oltramare in maintaining that the Buddhist conception of Nāmarūpa was from a certain date steadily tending towards the Sāṅkhya conceptions of the Puruṣa and Prakriti. It would be travelling too far from our immediate object to institute an enquiry into the relationship between the Buddhist philosophy and mode of self-realisation on one hand and the Yoga system on the other. Accepting as a working hypothesis that the relationship is in many respects very close, it requires no great effort of the imagination to realize how Buddhaghosa easily passed from the old to the new. The fact of Buddhaghosa being thus a connecting link between the two systems is enough to give him a very important place in the history of Indian Philosophy. Buddhaghosa enriched his Buddhist heritage with fresh materials from other systems; consider, for example, his use of the term, "Samūha," which reminds us at once of Patañjali's Mahābhāṣya. There are many other similar passages. The student of Buddhaghosa can judge for himself the great scholar's tender regard for his friends in Ceylon, his devotion to his teachers, his gratitude to his patrons, his meekness of spirit, his resourcefulness, his vast erudition and other traits which characterize a great teacher of mankind. Although it is not definitely known at what age he died, it is conceivable that he lived long enough to see his labours amply rewarded, enjoy the world-wide fame that he so well-deserved. He did not live in vain. As long as Buddhism remains a living faith among mankind Buddhaghosa will not cease to be remembered with reverence and gratitude by Buddhist peoples and schools. We shall touch just one more point before we conclude. Buddhaghosa is perhaps the greatest of celebrities of the Mahāvihāra at Anurādhapura, but it remains yet to determine his place in the history of the relation of Northern India with the Deccan. In the epilogue of his commentary on the Vinaya Piṭaka, he tells us that he completed his great work in the 21st year of the reign of King Sirinivāsa of Ceylon who was his benevolent royal patron. Perhaps he refers to the same king under the name of Sirikudda (Sirikūṭa) in the epilogue to his commentary on the Dhammapada.[1] It is left to further research to settle whether or not Sirinivāsa was another name of King Mahānāma, during whose reign he visited Ceylon according to the Mahāvaṁsa. The Revd. Bhikkhu H. P. Buddhadatta is of this opinion. He points out that nowhere else is mentioned a king of Ceylon by the name of Sirinivāsa or Sirikudda.

Buddhaghosa refers to King Duṭṭhagāmaṇī Abhaya,[2] the national hero of Ceylon, and to king Coranāga,[3] son of king Vaṭṭagāmaṇī. He also makes mention of a king Mahānāga whose munificient gifts in connection with the art of healing at Penambarigana had won for him a lasting fame ; King Mahānāga is perhaps no other than king Buddhadāsa, father of king Mahānāma mentioned in the Mahāvaṁsa (Chap. XXX, 171).

Thera Buddhadatta, another celebrity of the Mahāvihāra of Ceylon, was probably an older contemporary of Buddhaghosa. He was an inhabitant of Cola kingdom, situated below the Kāverī. He tells us that his royal patron was King Accutavikkanta of the Kalamba dynasty. All his works were written in the famous monas-

---

1 Dhammapada Commentary, Vol. IV, p. 235.

2 Atthasālinī, p. 80.

3 Ibid., p. 399.

tery erected by Veṇhudāsa or Kaṇhadāsa[1] on the banks of the Kāverī.

It is doubtful if the two teachers met each other either in India or elsewhere. They drew materials from the same source, no doubt. This fact can well explain why the Visuddhimagga and the Abhidhammāvatāra have so many points in common. In point of fact the two teachers wrote independently of each other. Nevertheless, whether prior or posterior, the Abhidhammāvatāra of Buddhadatta can be safely regarded as a catechism of the last portion of the Visuddhimagga. Buddhadatta, too, used the simile of the purblind and the lame as an analogy of the relation between nāma and rūpa.[2] Buddhadatta's division of terms into samūha and asamūha is another interesting point. It will be remembered that such a division of terms as this was far in advance of the older classifications embodied in the Puggala Paññatti commentary.[3] Supposing that Kumāra Gupta of the Imperial Gupta dynasty was a contemporary of King Mahānāma of Ceylon and that Buddhaghosa was a younger contemporary of Thera Buddhadatta, it follows that king Accutavikkanta of Kalamba Dynasty was a contemporary of Kumāra Gupta.

It is conceivable that the Buddhist monastery where Buddhaghosa met Thera Revata, was situated somewhere in South India, say, near the upper banks of the Godāvarī. Buddhaghosa's knowledge of South India below the Godāvarī is next to nothing.

The scene of Buddhaghosa's career as a scholar in India was confined between the Ganges on the north and

---

1 Buddhadatta's Manuals, Viññāpanaṁ, pp. xv, foll.

2 Abhidhammāvatāra (P.T.S.), p. 115.

3 Cf. Puggala Paññatti Commentary, P.T.S., p. 173.

the Godāvarī on the south. These two rivers were uppermost in his mind.[1] Elsewhere he defines southern provinces (Dakṣinajanapada) in the Deccan (Dakkhināpatha) as a tract of land lying to the south of the Ganges.[2] His personal acquaintance with the Āndhra countries is evident from his detailed account of an island in the midst of the Godāvarī.[3] In an interesting passage of the Sumaṅgala Vilāsinī, he has described apparently a local aboriginal custom of bleaching human bones.[4] Moreover we find in him anticipations of the Māyāvāda of Saṅkara. Matter summed up in terms of the four gross elements is unknowable. The impressions which we have of matter are mere appearances. If our hypothesis be true, it will be a most fruitful enquiry in the immediate future to determine how Thera Buddhaghosa was a connecting link between Northern India, the Deccan and Ceylon.

---

1 Atthasālinī, p. 140.

2 Sumaṅgala-Vilāsinī, I, p. 265.

3 Paramatthajotikā, II, p. 581.

4 Sumaṅgala-Vilāsinī, P.T.S., pt. I, "Dopanaṅti," p. 84.

CHAPTER V.

THE LICCHAVIS IN ANCIENT INDIA.

The mighty race of the Vajjians fills an important chapter in the ancient history of India. But unfortunately very few historians have up till now dealt with the subject with that thoroughness which it deserves. Their methods of administration, their martial spirit, above all, their nobility of character, are so impressive, so inspiring and so fascinating that it is really inexplicable how they escaped the attention of eminent scholars. Their cultural history is bound to be attractive. They had eight confederate clans of which the Licchavis of Vaiśālī were the most important. In this paper an attempt has been made to deal with some important topics relating to them.

The late Drs. V. A. Smith [1] and S. C. Vidyābhūṣaṇ [2] contributed two articles on the subject to the Indian Antiquary. According to Dr. Smith, the Licchavis were Tibetans in their origin. This conclusion he supports on two grounds: (*a*) the way in which they disposed of the dead, and (*b*) their judicial system. Dr. Vidyābhūṣaṇ, on the other hand, holds that the Licchavis were originally Persians, they having migrated from their original home at Nisibi and settled in India and Tibet. But neither of these theories will stand the test of a thorough critical examination.

Mr. Hodgson holds that they were Scythians.[3] It is

---

1 Ind. Ant. Vol. XXXII, pp. 233–236.

2 ,, ,, Vol. XXXVII, pp. 78–80.

3 Collected Essays by Hodgson (Trubner's edition), p. 17.

mentioned in the Vaijayantī that a Kṣatriya lady married to a Vrātya brings forth a Licchavi.[1] According to the lexicographers Amarasiṁha, Halāyudha and Hemacandra, they were Kṣatriyas and Vrātyas—sons of Kṣatriyas. Böhtlingk and Roth are of the opinion that they came of a regal race. Monier Williams supports this view.[2] The Dulva states[3] that when Moggallāna entered Vaiśālī in search of alms, the Licchavis were coming out of the city to subdue Ajātaśatru. Out of veneration they enquired whether they would be successful in a campaign against Ajātaśatru. Moggallāna replied, "Men of Vasiṣṭha's race, you will conquer." This proves that the Licchavis were Kṣatriyas, for we know that men of Vasiṣṭha's gotra are Kṣatriyas. It is mentioned in the Mahāparinibbāṇa Sutta of the Dīgha Nikāya[4] that the Licchavis claimed a portion of the relic of the august body of the Buddha as they were his castemen. It is stated there, "Bhagavā pi khattiyo, mayaṁ pi khattiyā" (Blessed one is a Kṣatriya, so are we). From these two instances, we can safely come to the conclusion that the Licchavis were Kṣatriyas. This is also corroborated by the Jaina account given in the Kalpasūtra.[5] It is stated there that Mahāvīra was a maternal uncle of the Licchavis and they illumined the city to commemorate his death. It may be interesting to note in this connection that a great famine broke out at Vaiśālī when Buddha was invited to check it. The

---

1 Vaijayantī (Oppert), p. 76, L. 108.

2 A Sanskrit English Dictionary by Monier Williams, p. 902. New edition 1899.

3 The Life of the Buddha, by Rockhill, p. 97, Footnote.

4 Dīghanikāya (P.T.S.), Vol. II, p. 164.

5 Kalpa Sūtra (Jacobi), Verse 128, p. 266, S.B.E., Vol. XXII.

chief queen of Benares became pregnant and was delivered of a lump of flesh. To avoid a scandal, she placed it in a pot and threw it into the Ganges, the pot drifting with the current. Gods took it and wrote on it that it contained the son of the chief queen of Benares. A hermit found the pot and kept it with him. From this lump of flesh children were born and they were known as the Licchavis.[1] This mythical account has very little historical value of its own.

As to the term Licchavi or Lecchavi, Chinese works point out that by it we understand 'skin.'[2] Buddhaghosa in his Paramatthajotikā on the Khuddaka Pāṭha[3] splits it up into līnā-chavi = Licchavi = Nicchavi. He says that things in their stomach appear to be attached to their chavi or skin and hence they are called Licchavis. ("Sibbetvā ṭhapitā viya nesaṁ aññamaññaṁ līnā ahosi.")

The young Licchavis of Vaiśālī were a free, wild people, very handsome and full of life. They dressed well and drove fast carriages.[4] Once Buddha with the Bhikkhus went out in search of alms. He addressed his followers when he saw the Licchavis on his way, "Look at the Licchavis, those who have not seen the Tāvatiṁsa gods, let them look at these Licchavis."[5] We know that the Tāvatimsa gods were very beautiful.[6]

It is stated in the Dulva[7] that there were continuous festivities among the Licchavis. Of them Chaṇa and

---

1 Paramatthajotikā (P.T.S.), pp. 158–165.

2 Watters' Yuan Chwang, Vol. II, p. 79.

3 Paramatthajotikā on Khuddaka-Pāṭha (P.T.S.), pp. 158–165.

4 Watters' Yuan Chwang, Vol. II, p. 79.

5 Mahāvastu, ed. Senart Vol. I, p. 262.

6 Buddhist Suttas (S.B.E.), Vol. XI, p. 32.

7 The Life of the Buddha by Rockhill, p. 63.

Sabbarattivāro were the most important. At the Sabbarattivāro or Sabbaratticāro festival, songs were sung, trumpets, drums and other musical instruments were used,[1] flags were flown, kings, princes and commanders-in-chief took part in the festival and spent the whole night in merry-making.

It is stated in the Dhammapadaṭṭhakathā that they used to go to gardens with prostitutes (Nagara-sobhinī) and enjoy themselves very much.[2]

Some young Licchavis were rude in manners.[3] They loved fine arts and built many beautiful caityas,[4] parks and gardens.[5] It is held that they were unbelievers in the Buddha and they had their Caityas consecrated to the Yakkhas.[6] This view is incorrect. It is evident from the Aṅguttara Nikāya[7] that they were devoted to Buddha. When Buddha was at Vaiśālī, 500 Licchavis worshipped him. It is stated in the Majjhima Nikāya[8] that some Licchavis saluted Buddha with folded hands as soon as he was seen by them. Some sat silent at a distance from the Blessed One. They were so very devoted to Buddha that they are said to have arranged a voyage for him by boat.[9]

They took delight in philosophical speculations about the non-cause of sins of beings, non-cause of the purity of beings,[10] nirvāṇa, lobha, dosa, moha, alobha, adosa

---

1 Samyutta Nikāya (P.T.S.), Vol. I, p. 201.
2 Dhammapadaṭṭhakathā, P T.S., Vol. III, pp. 279–280.
3 Watters' Yuan Chwang, Vol. II, p. 79.
4 Aṅguttara Nikāya (P.T.S.), Vol. IV, p. 309.
5 The Life of the Buddha by Rockhill, p. 63.
6 Beal's Life of Hiuen Tsiang. Introduction, p. xxiii.
7 Aṅguttara Nikāya, Vol. III, p. 239.
8 Majjhima Nikāya, Vol. I, 228.
9 Divyāvadāna (Cowell and Neil), pp. 55–56.
10 Samyutta Nikāya, Vol. III, pp. 68–71.

and amoha.[1] They discussed among themselves problems dealing with the destruction of action, destruction of sensation, means of attaining nirvāṇa, three kinds of sufferings, etc.[2] Abstruse metaphysical discussions relating to sīla, samādhi, paññā, vimutti, influence of the purity of sīla and tapa [3] and sublimity of dhamma [4] engaged their serious attention. They used also to discuss the five kinds of rare gems: hatthiratana assaratana, gahapatiratana, and itthiratana.[5] Dr. B. M. Barua holds in his Prolegomena to a study of Buddhist Philosophy [6] that the Vajjiputtakas recognise soul and their view of ātmā differs from the views of Sāṅkhya and the Vedānta. The Licchavis believed in spirits. They believed in the existence of hell, especially the Sattussadam Nirayam.[7]

They were fine sportsmen and accurate archers. They used to hunt with the help of dogs.[8] They used to kill animals on the 8th, 14th and 15th day of the lunar month and eat their flesh.[9] They were rough, cruel and haughty. Some young men among them were charged with insulting girls of respectable families by throwing stones at them.[10] They had the moral courage to confess their guilt.[11]

---

1 Samyutta Nikāya Vol. IV, pp. 261–262.

2 Aṅguttara Nikāya, Vol. I, pp. 220–222.

3 ,, ,, Vol. II, pp. 200–202.

4 ,, ,, Vol. III, pp. 75–78.

5 Aṅguttara Nikāya, Vol. III, pp. 167–168.

6 Dr. B. M. Barua's Prolegomena to a study of Buddhist Philosophy, p. 42.

7 Petavatthu (P. T. S.), p. 46.

8 Aṅguttara Nikāya (P.T.S.), Vol. III, pp. 75–78.

9 Divyāvadāna (Cowell and Neil), p. 136.

10 Aṅguttara Nikāya, Vol. III, pp. 75–78.

11 Cullavagga (S.B.E.), Vol. XX, pp. 118–125.

As regards the education of the Licchavis, we know that a Licchavi named Mahāli went to Taxila to learn śilpa and returned home after completion of training. He in his turn trained many other Licchavis who took up the same work and in this way education spread far and wide among the Licchavis.

It is mentioned in the Mahāparinibbāṇa Sutta of the Dīgha Nikāya that king Ajātaśatru of Magadha annihilated the Vajjians. Prof. Rhys Davids in his Buddhist India, p. 12, holds that it was some political motive which induced him to do so but the learned doctor is silent as to what that motive was. It seems that the Vajjians attacked Ajātaśatru many times and in order to baffle their attempts (Vajjinaṁ paṭibāhāya),[1] two of his ministers, Sunidha and Vassakāra built a fort at Pāṭaligāma. It is mentioned in the Dulva[2] that a Licchavi named Mahānāman lived at Vaiśālī who had a daughter named Amrapālī. According to the law of Vaiśālī, a perfect woman was not allowed to marry but was reserved for the enjoyment of the people. So Amrapālī became a courtesan. King Bimbisāra of Magadha came to know of this and himself went to Vaiśālī for her sake although he was at war with the Licchavis. Amrapālī had a son named Abhaya. Ajātaśatru was under the impression that his foster brother, Abhaya, had Licchavi blood in him and he liked the Licchavis very much. At this time the Licchavis were gaining strength day by day and Ajātaśatru thought that if Abhaya sided with them it would be very difficult for

---

1 Vajjinampatibāhāya. Some translate it thus—" to retard the progress of the Vajjians." The proper interpretations will be as follows—" to remove the Vajjians" ; " to drive away the Vajjians."

2 The Dulva quoted in The Life of the Buddha by Rockhill, p. 64.

him to cope with the Licchavis. So he made up his mind to do away with them.

In the Sumaṅgalavilāsinī,[1] we find that there was a port near the Ganges and there was a mountain not far from it and at the foot of the mountain there was a mine of precious gems. Some precious gems were washed away by the Ganges, and there was a contract between the Licchavis and Ajātaśatru that they would take the gems equally. But the avaricious Licchavis did not fulfil the agreement. This enraged Ajātaśatru very much. He thought of punishing them for this act. He realized, however, that the Licchavis being numerically stronger, he would fail to carry out his purpose. He tried to be friendly with the Licchavis, but he had to give up this idea. At last he resorted to the device of sowing dissensions and he was not unsuccessful. Through his machinations the unity of the Licchavis was almost broken with the result that the poor Licchavis began to hate the rich and the strong looked down upon the weak. At that psychological moment Ajātaśatru took advantage of the internal dissensions amongst the Licchavis and attacked the Vajjibhūmi. The weak Licchavis refused to stand against him and said, "Let the strong Licchavis go forward and crush him." Thus it was easy for Ajātaśatru to conquer Vaiśālī, the capital of the Vajjians.

If a Licchavi fell ill, the other Licchavis came to see him. The whole clan would join any auspicious ceremony performed in the house of a Licchavi. When a foreign king paid a visit to the Licchavi country, the

---

[1] Sumaṅgalavilāsinī (Burmese Edition, Simon Hewavitarne's Bequest Series No. 1 Revised by Ñānissara), p. 99.

Licchavis went out in a body to receive him and do him honour. They did not impose new taxes. Old taxes were abolished. The young Vajjians used to learn rājanīti from the old experienced Vajjians. Chastity was not to be violated by force. The old religious rites were observed. They used to hold frequent meetings. Matters relating to various parts of the country were heard and discussed. They sent out armies at the approach of foreign invaders. By beat of drum the meeting was announced and everyone tried to attend and having done their work they dispersed at the same time.[1]

A Licchavigaṇa could select a suitable wife for a Licchavi when asked for. It was for the Licchavigaṇa to decide cases of adultery.[2] Among the Licchavis of Vaiśālī, there was a law to the effect that a woman born in the first district[3] could marry only in the first district and not in the second or the third. One born in the middle district could marry only in the first and the second. One born in the third district could marry in any one of the three. Marriage outside Vaiśālī was not allowed.[4]

As regards the administration of justice when a thief is caught, he is brought before the Mahāmātto who can acquit him if he thinks him not guilty, but if he thinks him guilty he cannot inflict punishment upon him but can send him to Vohāriko who if he thinks that punishment is necessary, sends him to Antokāriko who in his turn sends him to Senāpati; and if he is convinced of his guilt, he sends him to Uparājā who again sends him

---

1 Sumaṅgalavilāsinī, Burmese Edition, pp. 103–105.

2 Bhikkhuṇivibhaṅga Sanghādidesa, Vol. II, p. 225.

3 Vaiśālī was divided into three districts.

4 The Life of the Buddha by Rockhill, p. 62.

to Rājā if he thinks him guilty. Rājā as the highest court of appeal could inflict punishment upon him according to the Paveṇipotthaka, i.e. Book of Precedents.[1]

The Licchavis had a republican form of government. Rājā was the highest court of appeal who alone could inflict punishment. He was elected by the people or rather by the ruling clans of the Licchavis. The administration of the country was in the hands of the Licchavigaṇa who elected their members. In the Licchavisaṅthāgāra, discussions were held on the Tīrataṇas. It is not mentioned in the Samantapāsādikā[2] that the Licchavi assembly was like the assembly of gods (Tāvatiṁsadevā). "In the assembly of the Tāvatiṁsa gods, four kings were the receivers of spoken words with regard to the matter for which the 33 gods met in the assembly and four great kings were the receivers of the admonition given."[3] From this Dr. Rhys Davids infers that the four great kings were regarded as Recorders (in their memory) of what had been said. The minutes of the meetings were kept by them. If so, there must have been such Recorders in the Mote halls of the clans.

Their relations with some ancient chiefs and tribes may be briefly noted : They were on friendly terms with King Pasenadī of Kośala as is evident from the account given in the Aṅgulimāla Sutta of the Majjhima N.[4] Pasenadī went to the Buddha and confessed that Bimbisāra of Magadha and the Licchavis were his friends.

The Mallas and the Licchavis were not on friendly

---

1 Sumaṅgalavilāsinī (Sinhalese Edition), Vol. I, p. 356.

2 Samantapāsādikā (Burmese edition), p. 338.

3 The Dialogues of the Buddha, p. 263.

4 Majjhima Nikāya, Vol. II, pp. 100–101.

terms. This is corroborated by the account of the fight between Bandhula, a Mallian general and the Licchavis.[1]

It is stated in the Cullavagga of the Vinaya Piṭaka[2] that Vaddha, a Licchavi was instigated to bring a false charge against Dabba, a Mallian, of breach of morality, but he confessed his guilt and was punished. The Licchavis had connections with the Imperial Guptas. Chandra Gupta I married Kumārdevī, the daughter of the Licchavis.

---

1 Faüsboll's, Dhammapada, p. 219 (Old edition).

2 S.B.E.., Vol. XX, p. 118.

CHAPTER VI.

BUDDHA AND NIGAṆṬHAS.

Introduction.

Jainism plays an important part in the history of India. This religion is no doubt older than Buddhism, as from all accounts it is clear that Mahāvīra, the last Tīrthaṅkara, was an older contemporary of the Buddha. The principles of Jainism have, according to tradition, existed in India from the earliest times. The names Ṛsabha, Nemi, etc., are well known in the Vedic Literature. But there is nothing to show that they were the Tīrthaṅkaras or the Jainas.

Reference to Jainism may be traced in the Mahābhārata; in the Ādiparva mention is made of Kṣapaṇaka.[1]

The members of the Jaina order are known as Nirgranthas (Nigaṇṭhas). Dr. Rhys Davids says, "The Jains have remained as an organised community all through the history of India from before the rise of Buddhism down to-day."[2] At the time of the Buddha Gautama, the Nirgranthas evidently formed a large and influential body. "The Jains had their ritual Code and their religious and philosophic creed and organisation at the time of the founder of Buddhism."[3]

As Mahāvīra was a native of Vaiśāli, the great city of the Licchavis, where the founder of Buddhism also spent

---

[1] Mahābhārata, Chapter III, S. 126—Nagṇaṁ kṣapanakaṁ "Kṣapanaka is a religious mendicant, specially a Jaina mendicant, who wears no garment. Monier-Williams' Sanskrit Dictionary, p. 326, 1899.

[2] Buddhist India, p. 143.

[3] Watters on Yuan Chwang, Vol. I, p. 252.

much of his time, and further as the two great teachers worked in the same provinces of Kośala, Magadha, Aṅga and Videha, it is but natural that the two sects would often come in contact with each other and we may expect the Buddhist religious books to contain references to the rival Saṅgha. The Buddhist records abound in incidental references to a number of teachers including Nigaṇṭha Nāthaputta and his doctrines are often scrutinised and sometimes discredited. But it is unfortunate that though the Buddhist works show traces of criticism of their doctrines, the two great teachers never appear to have met face to face; at least there is no authentic record of such a meeting. In the Buddhist books, there is a good deal of recrimination and fault-finding against the rival creed and every incident that is narrated contributes to the success of the writer's own faith. Sometimes we are confronted with the doubt whether the Buddhist books give a genuine version and interpretation of the Jaina dogmas that are criticised, and it is for Jaina scholars to test their accuracy. What we have attempted in this book, is to bring together the passages in Buddhist literature containing references to the last Jīna and to Jainism and leave it open to the followers of that religion to examine them in the light of their own records and the principles of their own faith.

The Niddesa, a work in the Pāli Tripiṭaka, gives us a list of disciples and devotees. Mention is made of the Nigaṇṭhas in it—"Nigaṇṭhasāvakānaṁ Nigaṇṭho devatā."[1] Nigaṇṭhas are called the recluses of the red class (lohitābhijāti) and they are also known as those wearing

[1] Culla Niddesa, pp. 173–174.

one garment (ekasāṭakā).[1] They were protected by the Buddhist Emperor Aśoka.[2] Nigaṇṭha Nāthaputta (identified with Mahāvīra), the 24th Tīrthaṅkara of the Jains, was a leader of the Jain Order, who was a citizen of Vaiśālī. He is described as the "head of an order, of a following, the teacher of a school, well known and of repute as a sophist, revered by the people, a man of experience, who has long been a recluse, old and well-stricken in years."[3] ("Saṅghī ceva gaṇī ca gaṇācariyo ca ñāto yasassī titthakaro sādhusammato bahujanassa rattaññū cīrapabbajito addhagato vayo anuppatto.")

Before the advent of Buddha Gautama, say the authors of the Buddhist books with a bigoted respect for their own master, Mahāvīra acquired fame but it faded away before the rising glory and dazzling brilliance of Buddha's career.

About the second century B.C. when the Greeks had occupied a fair portion of Western India, Jainism appears to have made its way amongst them and the founder of the sect appears also to have been held in high esteem by the Indo-Greeks as is apparent from an account given in the Milinda Pañho.[4] It is stated there that five hundred Yonakas, that is, Greeks, asked King Milinda (Menander) to go to Nigaṇṭha Nāthaputta, to put his problems before him and to have his doubts solved.

Nigaṇṭha Nāthaputta was engaged in rousing the sophistic activity with which Aṅga and Magadha were permeated, as it is evident from the Majjhima Nikāya.[5]

---

1 Aṅguttara Nikāya, Vol. III, p. 383—"Lohitābhijāti nāma Nigaṇṭhā ekasāṭakā tivadati," S.V. pt. I, p. 162.

2 Kern, Manual of Indian Buddhism, p. 112.

3 Dialogues of the Buddha, Vol. II, p. 66.

4 The Questions of Milinda, S. B. E., Vol. XXXV, p. 8.

5 Vol. II (P.T.S.), p. 2.

In the Divyāvadāna, we find an account of Nirgrantha Nāthaputta who was astounded by the supernatural power of the Buddha.[1]

In the Sabhiya Sutta of the Sutta Nipāta, we find that a wandering teacher named Sabhiya asked Buddha if he was younger in age than the six distinguished teachers and junior to them by renunciation. Samaṇa Gotama simply evaded the question by telling the wanderer that seniority went by wisdom and not by age.[2]

We have another important passage which definitely states the fact that Samaṇa Gotama was a younger contemporary of the six heretical teachers. The Sāmagāma Sutta of the M.N.,[3] and the Pāṭika Sutta of the Dīgha Nikāya[4] testify to the fact that Nigaṇṭha Nāthaputta predeceased Buddha by a few years. Dr. Hoernle conjectures that Mahāvīra died some five years before the Buddha.[5] It follows from the evidence of Abhayarājakumāra Sutta[6] of the M.N. that Mahāvīra was aware of the dissension between Buddha and Devadatta. In the opinion of Dr. Kern, the death of Bimbisāra took place when Buddha reached the age of seventy-two and that Devadatta's agitation against the Buddha must be dated some time after this event.[7]

Judging from these documentary evidences, Dr. Hoernle's conjecture would seem to have substantial historical accuracy.

The Nigaṇṭha of the Nātha clan holds that Nigaṇṭha

---

1 P. 143. 2 Sutta-Nipāta (P.T.S.), pp. 91–92.

3 Vol. II (P.T.S.), p. 243.

4 (P.T.S.), Vol. III.

5 Ājivikas (Hastings' Encyclopaedia of Religion and Ethics).

6 Majjhima Nikāya, Vol. I, p. 392.

7 Kern's Indian Buddhism, pp. 38–39.

means free from bonds.[1] According to Spence Hardy, Nigaṇṭha Nāthaputta (Mahāvīra) was called Nigaṇṭha because he declared that there was no science with which he was not acquainted.[2] We think that the Nigaṇṭhas were those who were free from knots, that is, those who were free from the ties and the bonds that keep men enchained to this world of woe and travail, and those who were free from all restraint and hindrance.

According to Mahāvīra, one should abstain from killing beings, from theft, from falsehood, from sensual pleasures from spirituous liquor and those who do not renounce these, go to hell. He is said to hold further that a person will suffer the consequences of whatever may preponderate as between an act and the forbearance from it, that is to say, if the period during which a man abstains from cruelty and homicide is of longer duration than the period during which he kills animals, he will not go to hell.[3] The Buddha was also the propounder of this view. In the account given in the Sāmaññaphala Sutta of the Dīgha Nikāya, Mahāvīra is said to have laid great stress on the four-fold self-restraints (Cātuyāma-saṁvara). The term is differently interpreted by the Buddha first, in relation to Mahāvīra and secondly, on his own account. In reference to Mahāvīra, the term is interpreted thus: "A Nigaṇṭha lives restrained as regards all water, restrained as regards all evils, all evils he has washed away and he lives suffused with a sense of evil held at bay. Such is the four-fold self-restraint and since he is thus tied with this four-fold bond, therefore is he the Nigaṇṭha (free from bonds) called Gatatto (whose

---

1 Dialogues of the Buddha, Vol. II, pp. 74–75.

2 Manual of Buddhism by Spence Hardy, p. 302.

3 Saṁyutta Nikāya, pt. IV, p. 317.

heart is gone, i.e. to the summit, to the attainment of his aim) or Yatatto (whose heart is kept down, i.e. under command) and Ṭhitatto (whose heart is fixed)."[1]

Buddha explained the term somewhat differently when he explained it on his own account. By the four-fold self-restraint, he meant the four moral precepts each of which is viewed in its four-fold aspect. With regard to the first of the four restraints, Buddhaghosa thought that the Jains did not drink cold water on the ground that there were souls in it. It is distinctly stated in the Sum. Vil,[2] that Mahāvīra was conscious of living beings present in cold water and it is for this reason one should not take cold water ("so kira sītodake sattasaññī hoti). In the Cūlasakuladāyī Sutta of the M.N.,[3] we read that according to Mahāvīra, the four precepts and self-privation are the recognised roads to the blissful state of the soul. The Jains were given to Tapa (austerity)[4] to a somewhat less degree as recorded in the Introduction to the Kassapasīhanāda Sutta of the Dīgha Nikāya.

According to Mahāvīra, (says the Sumaṇgala-Vilāsinī, a commentary of the Dīgha Nikāya by Buddhaghosa) the soul which has no form is conscious. (arupī attāsaññī).[5] He is said to hold further that the soul and the world (attā ca loko ca) are both eternal giving birth to nothing new; they are steadfast as a mountain peak, as

---

[1] Gatatto—According to Buddhaghosa, it means whose mind has reached the end, that is to say, has reached the attainment of his aim.

Yatatto—Whose mind is controlled.

Ṭhitatto—Whose mind is well-established.

(Sumaṅgala-Vilāsinī, p. 168).

[2] p. 168.

[3] Vol. II, pp. 35–36.

[4] Dialogues of the Buddha, Vol. II, p. 221.

[5] Sumaṅgala-Vilāsinī (P.T.S.), p. 119.

a pillar firmly fixed. One important problem which strikes us is whether according to the Jains, a person will be justified in taking life even for the purpose of food.

We read in the Sūtrakritāṅga that the hatthitāpasas were those who used to kill every year one elephant for the purpose of food, on the ground that thereby they minimised the slaughter of life.[1] The Brahmin law-givers prohibited the eating of certain varieties of fish and flesh. The Upālisutta of the M.N. contains an interesting discourse on this subject.[2] The Jaina householder Upāli pointed out that according to his master every act of killing is a cause of demerit whether the act be intentional or not. Buddha demurred to this view of Mahāvīra as he thought that man commits no sin when the act is unintentional. It is impossible, according to the Buddha, to abstain from killing, for even in moving about, a man is bound to kill many lives. The Jainas took exception to the Buddhist view and an interesting account of it is given in Sūtrakritāṅga.[3]

He (Mahāvīra) is said to hold the extraordinary view that a man must serve his own interest even if he has to kill his own father and mother. To refute this theory, Buddha said, "It is treachery to cut the branch of the tree that gives shade."[4] "Speak not of Karma but of Daṇḍa"—this was the view of Mahāvīra. According to him, there are said to be three causes of sin with regard to body, speech and thought. Each is distinct from the other.[5]

---

[1] Gaina Sūtras, pt. II, p. 418, Aupapātika Sutta (Edited by Leumann), p. 74.

[2] Vol. I, p. 377. [3] Pt. II, pp. 414–417.

[4] Jātaka, Vol. V, p. 123.

[5] Majjhima Nikāya, Vol. I, p. 372.

While staying at Rājagriha, Buddha said to Mahānāma, "once some Nigaṇṭhas were suffering lying on earth by the side of Isigili. One evening I approached and enquired why they were thus suffering lying on earth. They replied that their Nāthaputta who was all-knowing, all-seeing, had told them that they had in their previous birth, performed sinful acts for which they would have to suffer, and to annihilate the sinful acts, they would have to live restrained in body, mind and speech; and future sins would be annihilated."

"On the destruction of sin, misery will be destroyed, on the destruction of misery, there will be the extinction of Vedanā (suffering). On the extinction of suffering, all sorts of misery will be eradicated." They further said that they believed in and accepted this instruction. Such instruction was wholesome to them. Then I asked them whether they were aware of the fact of their sinning in their previous births. They answered in the negative. I said, "You do not know what sins you have committed and what those sins are, then knowing nothing why do you torture yourself for sin." They said, "Happiness cannot be obtained through happiness, one has to labour hard for happiness." "At last the Buddha made them understand fully."[1]

Sīha, a disciple of Nigaṇṭha Nāthaputta and the Buddha.

After Mahāvīra had developed his doctrines and preached his creed of unbounded charity to all living beings in the Vajji land and in Magadha, the number of his followers among the Licchavis steadily grew larger and among them there were some men of the highest position in Vaiśāli. This appears from the Buddhist books themselves.

[1] Majjhima Nikāya (P.T.S.), Vol. I, pp. 92–93.

In the Mahāvagga of the Vinaya Piṭaka, we read that Sīha, the General-in-Chief of the Licchavis, was a disciple of Nigaṇṭha Nāthaputta (who has been shown by Drs. Bühler and Jacobi to be identical with Mahāvīra of the Jaina legends). We read how General Sīha, the follower of the Nigaṇṭhas, became gradually attracted towards the Samaṇa Gotama by listening to the discussion among the Licchavis at the Saṅthāgāra or Mote-Hall, where they used to meet, discuss and settle all matters relating to politics or religion.

One day many distinguished Licchavis were sitting together, assembled in the Mote-Hall, and they spoke in many ways in praise of the Buddha, Dhamma and Saṁgha. At that time, Sīha was sitting in that assembly and he thought thus, "Truly he, the Blessed One, must be the Arahat Buddha, since these many distinguished Licchavis who are sitting here together assembled in the Mote-Hall speak in so many ways in praise of the Buddha, the Dhamma, and the Saṁgha." Sīha next asked permission to visit the Buddha from Nigaṇṭha Nāthaputta who however tried to dissuade him from doing so, pointing out the defects in the doctrines preached by the former. "Why should you, Sīha, who believe in the result of the actions or Kiriyavāda, according to their moral merits, go to visit the Samaṇa Gautama who denies the result of actions; he teaches the doctrines of non-action, and in this doctrine he trains his disciple."

Siha's enthusiasm for the Buddha abated for the time being but it was again roused by the discussion of the other Licchavis, so that he at last did pay a visit to the Buddha who gave him a long discourse on the Buddhist doctrines. Sīha was at last converted to the Buddhist faith. That the number of followers of Mahāvīra at Vaiśālī however was very large, also appears from this story of Sīha. This general invited the Buddha and the Bhikkhus to take their meals at his house and brought meat from the market for feeding them. But the Jains spread a false report as we read in the Mahāvagga: "At that time a great number of the Nigaṇṭhas (ruṇning) through Vaiśālī, from road to road, cross-way to cross-way, with outstretched arms cried, "To-day Sīha, the General, has killed a great ox and has made a meal for the Samaṇa Gautama, the Samaṇa Gotama (Gautama) knowingly eats this meat of an animal killed for this very purpose, and has thus become virtually the author of that deed (of killing the animal)."[1] This false report circulated by them made Sīha firmer in his zeal for the new faith, but the story shows that the number of the Nirgraṇthas at Vaiśālī was sufficiently large to defy the influence of such a great man as Sīha, and the fact that the conversion of Sīha took place at the time when Buddha paid his last visit to the city shows that though Buddha had made many converts among the followers of the faith preached by Mahāvīra, yet they were still numerous and powerful at the capital of the Licchavis despite the numerous sermons preached by the Buddha. This is also confirmed by the story of Saccaka, a Nirgraṇtha, who had the hardihood to challenge the Buddha himself to a discussion on philosophical tenets before an assemblage of five hundred Licchavis.

Saccaka and the Buddha.

When the Blessed One was at Vaiśālī, five hundred Licchavis assembled in the Saṅthāgāra on account of some business. Nigaṇṭhaputta, Saccaka

[1] Vinaya Texts, S.B.E., Vol. XVII, p. 116.

approached the place where the Licchavis were and said to the Licchavis "Let the Licchavis come out to-day; I shall hold a conversation with Samaṇa Gautama. If the Samaṇa Gotama places me in the same position in which I am placed by the monk Assaji who is a Sāvaka, I shall defeat Samaṇa Gotama by my argument like a strong man catching hold of a goat by its long hair and moving it in any way he likes." Saccaka mentioned the various ways in which he was going to treat Samaṇa Gotama. Some Licchavis enquired thus, "How will Samaṇa Gotama meet the argument of Saccaka, a Nigaṇṭhaputta and vice versa" while others enquired how Nigaṇṭhaputta Saccaka would meet the arguments of Samaṇa Gotama and vice versa. Saccaka induced five hundred Licchavis to go with him to listen to the discussion with Gotama. He approached the place where the Bhikkhus were walking up and down and asked them, "We are anxious to see Gotama, the Blessed One." The Buddha was seated to spend the day in meditation at the foot of a tree in the Mahāvana forest. Nigaṇṭhaputta Saccaka with a large number of Licchavis went to the Blessed One and having exchanged friendly greetings with him, sat at a little distance. Some Licchavis saluting him took their seats, others exchanged friendly greetings and then took their seats, some saluting with folded hands sat at a little distance, some prominent Licchavis giving out their names and family names took their seats at a little distance. Some remained silent and sat at a little distance with great devotion to the Blessed One. Then arguments relating to the Saṅghas and Gaṇas, some knotty points of Buddhist psychology and some knotty metaphysical questions were started between Saccaka and the Blessed One. Saccaka being defeated invited the Blessed One who accepted the invitation. The Licchavis were informed of this and asked to bring whatever they liked at the dinner which would be held on the following day. At break of day, the Licchavis brought five hundred dishes for the Buddha.[1] Saccaka together with the Licchavis became greatly devoted to the Blessed One.

Among the males and females who attained distinction as theras and theris, i.e. brothers and sisters and whose impassioned utterances have been preserved among the Psalms of the Brethren and the Psalms of the Sisters, we find some who had come in contact with the rival faith of the Nigaṇṭhas and are said to have been converted from Jainism to Buddhism. The history of their lives is given in Dhammapāla's Paramatthadīpanī on the Thera and the Therigāthā.

Nanduttarā, born of a Brahmin family in the kingdom of the Kurus, learnt arts and sciences and entered the order of the Nigaṇṭhas. She in the course of her journey once met Mahāmoggallāna and she was defeated in a discourse. Being instructed she entered the order and very soon attained Arahatship 'thoroughly realising the meaning of the Norm.'[2]

Bhaddā, born in the family of the king's treasurer, entered the order of the Nigaṇṭhas. But she was dissatisfied with their doctrines. At the gate of some village, a branch of a rose-apple tree was set up by her, saying, "whoever is able to join issue with me in debate, let him trample on this bough." Sāriputta trampled the bough and in due course a debate ensued

---

[1] M.N., P.T.S., Vol. I, pp. 225–226.

[2] Psalms of the Sisters, pp. 57–58.

but she got puzzled. She said, "I know not, Lord!" The Lord taught her the Norm and she entered the order and attained saintship.[1]

Ajjuna, reborn in the family of a councillor at Śrāvastī, entered the order of Jains hoping to attain salvation. He was not satisfied; he met the Buddha, entered His Order and gradually became an Arahat.[2]

Abhaya was reborn as the son of King Biṃbisāra. Nāthaputta, the Jain leader, "taught him a dilemma to set the Samaṇa Gotama but in the master's reply he recognised the defeat of the Jain and the supreme enlightenment of the Exalted One." After the death of the king, Abhaya left home and entered the Buddhist Order. Gradually he reached the First Path; and at last he realised Arhatship.[3]

Sirigupta and Garahadinna.

There were in Srāvaśtī two friends named Sirigupta and Garahadinna. Sirigupta was a worshipper of the Buddha and Garahadinna was a disciple of the Jain Order. Every day Garahadinna used to say to Sirigupta, "Well, are you going to Samaṇa Gotama? What do you get from him? We go to the Nigaṇṭhas and give what ought to be given and receive what ought to be received, should you not do this?" Garahadinna heard some other persons say this to Sirigupta who was also told thus, "My friend, why do you go to Samaṇa Gotama? What do you get there? Should you not go to my master and make an offering to him?" For a long time Sirigupta was silent; then one day he said, "You always come and ask me to go and make offerings to your teachers instead of going and making offerings

1 Psalms of the Sisters, pp. 63–67.

2 Psalms of the Brethren, p. 83.

3 Ibid., p. 30.

to Samaṇa Gotama. I say, what do your teachers know ?" Garahadinna said, "Oh ! don't say that ; our teachers know everything, there is nothing unknown to them. All matters, present, past or future, all deeds, physical, verbal and mental and what would happen or would not happen—all these are known to them." Sirigupta said, "Do you speak of these words truly ?" Garahadinna said, "Yes, I do." Then Sirigupta said, "You have done a wrong by not telling me everything so long. Now I come to know the wisdom of your teachers, I shall go ; on my behalf, please invite the teachers." Then Garahadinna went to the teachers, saluted them and said, "Sirigupta has invited you for to-morrow." The teachers enquired whether Sirigupta himself had told him this. Garahadinna said, "Yes, my lords !" On hearing this, the teachers were greatly pleased and said, "Our mission has been fulfilled, if Sirigupta be pleased with us, then there would be nothing unobtainable for us."

Sirigupta got between the two large houses of his a hole dug and had it filled with filth and mud and outside the pit had thorny branches planted, and the four corners tied with rope in such a way that any one while sitting on the seat, would stumble down into the pit full of filth. He then spread a covering over the pit so that his device might not be discovered from the outside. Outside the house he kept empty pots with mouths covered with plantain leaves. He besmeared the pots with rice and ghee so that people might think that an arrangement on a lavish scale had been made for the wanderers. The following morning Garahadinna enquired whether everything had been made ready for the teachers. People who were present there said that everything had been done. He praised them and went away. On his departure five hundred Nigaṇṭhas came there. Sirigupta came out, stood with folded hands and thus thought within himself, " Your pupil Garahadinna has told me that you know the present, past and future, if you do not know this, you should not enter my house, there is no rice, or clarified butter ready in my house ; if you enter my house without knowing this, I shall put you all into the pit." Then he hinted to his servants to draw the covering in such a way that no filth might stick to it ; his servants asked the Nigaṇṭhas to come in ; they entered the house and were told to take pots individually and take seats. No sooner did they take their seats than the servants in compliance with the aforesaid hint, drew the covering and all of them fell into the pit full of mud and filth. Garahadinna was sorely grieved, went to the king and requested him to punish him with a heavy fine ; Sirigupta too went to the king and spoke out everything and paid the fine. Then again, Sirigupta began to behave like a friend as before. Garahadinna thought of harassing Sirigupta's master in this way and invited Buddha through Sirigupta and put ashes into a pit and spread a covering over it. The Buddha who was invited along with five hundred Bhikkhus, thought of this trick of Garahadinna and knowing that Sirigupta and Garahadinna would attain saintship, he went there ; as soon as he placed his leg on the seat, a lotus blossomed ; the empty vessels became full by the power of his miracle. With five hundred Bhikkhus the Buddha ate his fill and instructed everybody in the Dhamma. To see how the Buddha would be harassed, many people came there, but seeing this miracle they began to respect the Buddha. Many persons holding right views went there; they were glad to listen to the Buddha's instructions. Sirigupta and Garahadinna became Arahats.[1]

The Buddha and Dīghatapassī, a Jaina.

Once the Buddha was staying in a mango-grove in Nālandā. Dīghatapassī, a Nigaṇṭho, after dinner, went to him in the mango-grove, and after exchanging with him the compliments of friendship and civility, stood on one side. On the Lord asking him to take a seat, Dīghatapassī, a Nigaṇṭho sat on a comparatively low seat. Then the Lord said, "How many are the ways of creating sinful acts and the existence of sin?" In reply to this, he said, "We do not declare anything as sin, but we declare penalty only." It was asked by the Buddha thus, "Then how many kinds of penalty do the Nigaṇṭhas declare?"

The Nigaṇṭho said, "There are three kinds of penalty—penalty inflicted on body, on speech and on mind." "Are these three sorts of penalty distinct from one another?" "Yes, they are." "Which of these three is the most sinful?" "Of these three, the Nigaṇṭhas declare body-penalty as the most sinful." Then the Nigaṇṭho said to the Lord, "How many penalties does the Lord declare that give rise to sin?" The Lord said, "I do not declare anything as penalty, I declare Kamma (deed)." The Nigaṇṭho said, "Then you declare that as kāyakammam, vacikammam and manokammam which we declare as kāyadaṇḍo, vacidaṇḍo, and manodaṇḍdo: very well, which of the three kammas do you declare the most sinful?"

---

[1] Dhammapadaṭṭhakathā, Vol. I, pt. 2, pp. 434–447.

The Lord said, "I declare manokammam as the most sinful." Thus the discourse ended ; Dīghatapassī returned to his place. On being asked by the householder Upāli, he said that he had returned from the Lord Buddha and told him all about the discourse which he had with the Buddha. Then Upāli went to the Lord, and said, "Is it reasonable that you should declare Manadaṇḍo as the most sinful ?" "How is it that manakammo is more sinful than the gross Kāyakamma ?" The Lord said, "The act of killing animals cannot be performed unless the propensities of killing arise in one's mind. So in every act, mind is the principal factor, and mind precedes all acts, good and bad. All acts virtuous or vicious originate from mind, so why should not manakamma be more sinful than kāyakamma ?"

Buddha and Upāli.

Thus the Lord dispelled the doubt of Upāli by various reasonable arguments. Then Upāli said, "From this day forth, I become a member of the (Buddhist) saṁgha and accept the doctrine of the Buddha."

Dīghatapassī came to know all about Upāli but could not believe that Upāli had entered the Buddhist Order. He said this to Nigaṇṭha Nāthaputta and told him that it was necessary for them to go to Upāli. Thus advised, they with many followers went to Upāli who took the best seat and asked the Nigaṇṭhas to take their seats. At this Nigaṇṭha Nāthaputta said to Upāli, "You have run mad." Upāli said, "I have not run mad." "By the grace of the Lord Buddha, I have been able to know the real path to salvation ; my eyes are now open, you can never cause me to forget it." [1]

[1] Majjhima Nikāya, Vol. I, pp. 371–387.

Abhayarājakumāra and the Buddha.

Once the Buddha was staying at Kālaṇḍakanivāpa in Veluvana in Rājagriha. At that time Abhayarājakumāra went to Nigaṇṭha Nāthaputto, saluted him and took his seat on one side. Then Nāthaputta said to Abhaya, "You may be famous, if you can defeat Samaṇa Gotama by argument." He then taught Abhaya the questions to be put to Gautama, "Do you use any word that is harsh and unwholesome to others?" If the Lord answers in the affirmative, then ask him what difference is there between him and others; but if, he answers in the negative, then ask him the reason of his using the words, "Āpāyiko Devadatto, Nerayiko Devadatto, etc."

After this, Abhaya with a view to put questions to Gautama, invited him and came home. The following day, Gautama went to Abhaya's house. Abhaya fed him to his satisfaction, and reproduced to Gautama the questions taught by Nigaṇṭha Nāthaputta. Then the Lord said, "Whatever Tathāgata says is true, real and sweet; he does not say what is false, unreal and bitter. He uses, in some places, for a moment, unhappy words though true and real."

Thus Abhaya was pleased to have good advice full of sound reason from the Buddha and he came to have faith in the Buddha, the Dhamma and the Saṁgha.[1]

Visākhā.

Visākhā was the daughter of Dhanañjayaseṭṭhi, son of Meṇḍakaseṭṭhi, who lived in the city of Bhaddiya in the kingdom of Aṅga. The family of Meṇḍaka was greatly devoted to the Buddha. Dhanañjayaseṭṭhi, at the request of Pasenadī, King of Kosala, went to his kingdom and

[1] Majjhima Nikāya (P.T.S.), Vol. I, pp. 392 foll.

settled at Sāketa. Visākhā was married to Puṇṇavaddhana, son of Migārasetṭhi. Migārasetṭhi was a follower of the Niganṭhas. After marriage, she went to live with her father-in-law at Sāvatthī. One day Migārasetṭhi invited five hundred naked ascetics (niganṭhas) and when they came he asked his daughter-in-law to come and salute the Arahats. She came hearing about the Arahats and seeing them, she said, "Such shameless creatures can't be Arahats. Why my father-in-law has called me?" Saying this she blamed her father-in-law and went to her residence. The naked ascetic seeing this, blamed the Seṭṭhi and asked him to turn her out of the house as she was a follower of Samaṇa Gautama. But the Seṭṭhi knowing that it was not possible to do so apologised to them and sent them away. After this incident, the Seṭṭhi sitting on a valuable seat was drinking milk porridge with honey from a golden pot and Visākhā stood there fanning him. At that time a Buddhist monk entered the house for alms and stood before him but the Seṭṭhi took no notice of him. Seeing that Visākhā said to the thera, "go to another house, Sir, my father-in-law is eating stale fare." At this the banker grew angry. He then stopped eating and ordered his men to drive her out. Thereupon Visākhā said that he should examine her shortcomings. The Seṭṭhi welcomed the idea and summoned her relations and told them that his daughter-in-law had said to a Buddhist monk that he was eating stale food while he was drinking milk porridge with honey. Visākhā's relations enquired about the truth of the statement. Visākhā said that she did not say so. She only said that her father-in-law was enjoying the fruition of his merit in the previous birth. In this way Visākhā explained away everything that was considered by her father-in-law to bring blame upon her. While she was found not guilty by her relations, she prepared to leave the house of her father-in-law. Thereupon the banker apologised and entreated his daughter-in-law to remain in his house. She however consented to remain on one condition only, namely, that she could be allowed to entertain the Bhikkhus in the house at her will. The next day she invited the Buddha to her house. The naked ascetics knowing that the Buddha had entered the house of Migāraseṭṭhi surrounded the house. Visākhā requested her father-in-law to come and serve the Buddha himself. The naked ascetics prevented him going there. Thereupon Visākhā herself served the Buddha and his disciples and when their meal was finished, she again requested her father-in-law to come and listen to the sermon of the Buddha. The naked ascetics again said that it was extremely improper to go at that time but when he went to listen to the Buddha's sermon, the naked ascetics had gone there earlier and placed the curtain and requested the Seṭṭhi to sit outside it. The Seṭṭhi sat outside the curtain, listened to the Buddha's sermon, obtained the fruition of the first stage of sanctification, went up to his daughter-in-law and said to her, "Henceforward, you are my mother." From that time Visākhā came to be known as Migāramātā or Migāra's mother. Migāra was converted to Buddhism. Visākhā afterwards made a vihāra at Sāvatthī at the cost of twenty-seven crores of coins. (See Visākhā Vatthu, Dhammapadaṭṭhakathā (P.T.S.), Vol. I, pt. II, pp. 384 foll.)

Printed at the Baptist Mission Press, Calcutta.

INDEX.

Accutavikkanta, 63, 64.
Adhiccasamuppāda, 37, 38.
Adosa, 69.
Aggañña, 16.
Ahetuappaccayavāda, 37.
Aitareya Āraṇyaka, 40.
Ajātasatru, 71, 72.
Ajatatto, 30.
Ajita, 16.
Ajitakesakambalī, 27, 35, 36, 38, 42.
Ajjuna, 5, 88.
Akaraṇavāda, 37.
Akiriyavāda, 33, 36, 41.
Akkhaṇavedī, 5.
Alambanamantaṁ, 7.
Alobha, 69.
Aṅga, 7, 19, 93.
Anikyavāda, 33.
Annabhāra, 17, 19
Aññaṁsarīravādo, 33.
Antarakalpas, 39.
Anupiya, 16.
Anurādhapura, 59, 63.
Arthakāras, 29.
Arthaśāstra, 14, 15.
Asamūha, 64.
Aśoka, 26, 53.
Assaji, 86.
Aśvaghosa, 6.
Atharvaveda, 2.
Avijjā, 61.
Abhaya, 71, 88, 93.
Abhidharmakoṣa, 53.
Abhidharmamahāvibhāsaśāstra. 53.
Ājivika, 25, 29, 32, 33.
Ānanda, 16, 51.

Bahudantiputra, 14.
Bandhula, 75.
Bimbisāra, 1, 74.
Brahmadatta, 3.
Brihaspati, 14.
Buddha, 17, 18, 19, 20, 22, 24, 26, 27, 34, 35, 36, 67, and 84.
Buddhadatta, 59, 63, 64.
Buddhaghosa, 28, 38, 43, 44, 45, 49, 51, 55, 56, 57, 58, 59, 61, 62, 63, 64, 65, 68, 81.
Buddhist Canon, 26.
Bhaddā, 87.
Bhaddiya, 93.
Bhagavat Gītā, 33, 34.
Bhaggavagotta, 16.
Bharadvāja, 14.
Bharata, 7.
Bhīmsena, 3, 4, 71, 88.

Caityas, 69.
Campā, 7, 45.
Cātuyāmasaṁvara, 28, 30, 80.
Ceylon, 44, 57.
Cola kingdom, 63.
Coranāga, 63.
Cūlasakuladāyi, 19.
Chandragupta, 1, 75.
Chānakya, 14, 15.

Deccan, 51, 63, 65.
Devadatta, 25, 79, 93.
Dhammapadaṭṭhakathā, 1, 69.
Dhanañjayaseṭṭhi, 93.
Dharmakāras, 29.
Dīghabhānakas, 56.
Dīghatapassi, 91.
Dosa, 69.

Dulva, 67, 68.
Duṭṭhagāmaṇi Abhaya, 63.

Ekasāṭaka, 18, 78.
Epicurus, 35.

Ganges, 64, 72.
Ganthakāra monastery, 59.
Gardhavālī, 42.
Garhadinna, 88, 89, 90.
Gatatto, 30, 80.
Gāndhāra, 7.
Gijjhakūṭa, 16, 19.
Godāvarī, 64, 65.
Gosāla, Maṅkhaliputta, 21, 25.
Gotama, 43, 47.
Gupta dynasty, 64.
Guzerat, 2.
Gymnosophists, 42.
Ghosagāma, 59.
Ghoṭamukha, 14.

Halāyudha, 67.
Hatthimaṅgala, 6.
Hatthitāpasa, 30.
Hemchandra, 67.
Heretical teachers, 21.
Hiuen Tsiang, 53.
Hodgson, 66.
Hoernle, 79.
Hughli, 1.

India, 64.
Indo-Greeks, 78.
Itivādapāmokkha, 17.

Jacobi, 21, 22.
Jaina Bhagavatī, 21, 38.
Jambudīpa, 6.
Janaka, 11.
Jaṭilaka, 11.
Jīna, 39.
Jīvaka, 1.
Jñānaprasthānaśāstra, 53, 54.

Kaccāyana, 34, 35.
Kaikeyī, 7.
Kalpas, 39.
Kāmasūtra, 14.
Kaṇhadāsa, 64.
Kaniṣka, 53.
Kaunapadanta, 14.
Karma, 82.
Kātyāyana, 14, 34.
Kāverī, 63, 64.
Kāyadaṇḍo, 91.
Kāyakamma, 91, 92.
Kern, 25, 27.
Kesī, 59.
Khaggaratana, 4.
Khemā, 51.
Kokanuda, 17.
Kośala, 1, 74, 93.
Kosāmbi, 16.
Kṣapanaka, 76.
Kṣatriya, 67.
Ksemendra, 8.
Kumāradevī, 75.
Kumāra Gupta, 64.
Kunāla, 8.

Lakkhanahāra, 51.
Lāḷha, 1.
Lecchavi, 68.
Licchavigaṇa, 73, 74.
Licchavis, 66, 67, 68, 72, 76, 84, 86.
Lohitābhijātī, 77.

Magadha, 1, 7, 19, 24, 71, 74, 78, 83.
Mahākaccāyana, 45, 55, 56.
Mahākassapa, 45.
Mahākoṭṭhita, 45, 50, 51.
Mahāli, 71.
Mahāvīra, 21, 22, 24, 26, 27, 28, 30, 34, 35, 36, 41, 78, 80, 81, 85.

Mahinda, 44, 45.
Majjhimabhānakas, 56.
Makkhali Gosāla, 26, 30, 37, 38, 39, 40, 41.
Makkhali Gosālaputta, 23, 26, 32.
Mallas, 74.
Mallikā, 16.
Mallikārāma, 18.
Manodaṇḍo, 91.
Manokamma, 91, 92.
Maskarins, 25, 29.
Māgandiya, 19.
Māṅavas, 14.
Māyāvāda, 65.
Menander, 55.
Meṇḍakaseṭṭhi, 93.
Migāraseṭṭhi, 94, 95.
Milinda-Pañho, 23, 78.
Moggallāna, 26, 45, 67.
Moliyasīvako, 17, 18.

Naciketā, 33.
Nagarasobhinī, 69.
Nandiyo, 18.
Nanduttara, 87.
Nāgasena, 55, 61.
Nālandā, 45, 91.
Nāmarūpa, 61, 62.
Ñānodaya, 59.
Nārāca, 5.
Nemi, 76.
Niddesa, 66.
Nidhiuddharaṇamantaṁ, 7.
Nigaṇṭha Nāthaputta, 19, 77, 84, 93.
Nigaṇṭhas, 25, 76, 80.
Nirvāṇa, 18.
Nisibi, 66.
Northern India, 57, 63.

Oldenberg, 21.
Oltramare, M. 62.

Pakativāda, 56, 61.
Pakudhakātyāyana, 33.
Paramavaṇṇoattā, 19.
Pasenadī, 1, 14, 74, 93.
Patañjali, 57, 58, 61, 62.
Paṭisambhidā, 50.
Paṭṭhāna, 53.
Paveṇipotthaka, 74.
Pāyāsi, 36.
Pātimokkha, 43.
Pāvā, 45.
Penambarigaṇa, 63.
Permenedian doctrine, 33.
Persians, 66.
Pharusavācā, 28.
Pippalāda, 34, 37.
Pisuṇa, 14.
Pisuṇaputra, 14.
Pāṭaliputta, 47.
Potaliyo, 17.
Poṭṭhapāda, 13, 15, 16.
Prasnopanishat, 34.
Puggala Paññatti, 31.
Pūraṇakassapa, 20, 27, 36, 37, 38.
Puskala, 7.
Pyrrho, 42.

Raghuvaṁsa, 7.
Rājā, 74.
Rājagaha, 16, 17, 18, 19, 45.
Rājagṛiha, 83, 93.
Rāmāyaṇa, 8.
Recorders, 74.
Revata, 44, 57, 58, 59, 64.
Rhys Davids, 10, 38, 43, 76.
Rig Veda, 2.
Roth, 67.
Rṣabha, 76.

Sabbaratticāra, 69.
Sabbarattivāro, 69.
Sabhiya, 20, 24.

Saccaka, 32, 85, 86.
Saddavedhī, 5.
Sajjho, 17.
Sakuladāyī, 18.
Samantapāsādikā, 74.
Saṃgha, 77, 93.
Sammiddhi, 47, 48.
Samphappalāpa, 13.
Samūha, 62, 64.
Saṇḍaka, 16.
Sandhiyuttatuṇhiraṁ, 5.
Sanghadeva, 53.
Sanghapāla, 59.
Sañjaya Belaṭṭhiputta, 26, 41, 42.
Sañjaya, the wanderer, 41.
Saṅkara, 57, 65.
Sāṅkhya, 33, 34, 37, 56, 61.
Sannāhakañcukaṁ, 5.
Saṅthāgāra, 85.
Sarabho, 17.
Saralaṭṭhi, 5.
Saramaṇḍapa, 5.
Sarapaduma, 5.
Sarapāsāda, 5.
Sararajjuṁ, 5.
Saravanaṁ, 5.
Saravedhī, 5.
Sassatavāda, 33.
Suttussadaṁ Nirayaṁ, 70.
Sāketa, 17, 94.
Sāriputta, 26, 41, 42, 44, 45, 49, 50, 52, 70.
Sāsanapaṭṭhāna, 53.
Sāvatthī, 16, 17, 18, 45.
Scythians, 66.
Senāpati, 73.
Shaiva System, 34.
Sīha, 83.
Sīla, 70.
Sīlakkhandavagga, 13.
Śilpa, 71.
Sirigupta, 88, 89, 90.
Sirikudda, 63.
Sirinivāsa, 63.
Smith, V. A., 66.
South India, 64.
Spence Hardy, 21, 80.
Śrāvastī, 88.
Sucimukhī, 18.
Sunakkhatta, 16.
Sunidha, 71.
Sutavā, 17.

Tākākusu, 54.
Takkhasilā, 7.
Tāvatiṁsa gods, 68.
Taxila, 1, 3, 4, 71.
Tedaṇḍikas, 12.
Theravādins, 44, 56.
Ṭhitatto, 30, 81.
Thomas, F. W., 28.
Tikkha, 7.
Timbaruka, 18.
Tīrthaṅkara, 78.
Tissa, 53.
Titthiyas, 12.

Uddālaka Āruṇi, 10.
Uggahamāna, 15, 18.
Ujjainī, 45.
Ulumpā, 45.
Upālī, 92.
Upanishad, 33.
Uparājā, 73.
Uposatha, 7.
Usabha, 6.
Uttiyo, 17.

Vacchagotta, 18, 19.
Vacidaṇḍo, 91.
Vacikammo, 91, 92.
Vaijayantī, 67.
Vaiśālī, 66, 67, 72.
Vaiseṣika, 33.

Vajjians, 66, 71, 72.
Vajjiputtakas, 70.
Varadhara, 17, 19.
Varṇāśramadharma, 12.
Vasiṣṭha, 67.
Vassakāra, 71.
Vasuvandhu, 53.
Vaṭṭagāmaṇi, 63.
Vātavyādhi, 15.
Vātsyāyana, 14.
Vāyupurāṇa, 8.
Vedallas, 52.
Vedānta, 33, 70.
Vedas, 45, 60.
Videha, 77.
Vijjás, 2, 4.
Vimutti, 70.
Vinaya, 60.
Visākhā, 93, 94, 95.
Vohāriko, 13.
Vrātya, 67.

Yajurveda, 2.
Yakkhas, 69.
Yatdricchā, 37.
Yati, 32.
Yāgñavalkya, 10.
Yoga system, 56, 61, 62.
Yonakas, 78.

Zendāvestā, 40.

ERRATA.

Page	2	Read	From	Instead of	For
,,	16	,,	he	,,	they
,,	31	,,	account	,,	acount
,,	32	,,	Ājivika	,,	Ājivikas
,,	84	,,	doctrine	,,	doctrines
,,	91	,,	manodaṇḍo	,,	manodaṇḍdo
,,	93	,,	if	,	if,
,,	94	,,	ascetics	,,	ascetic